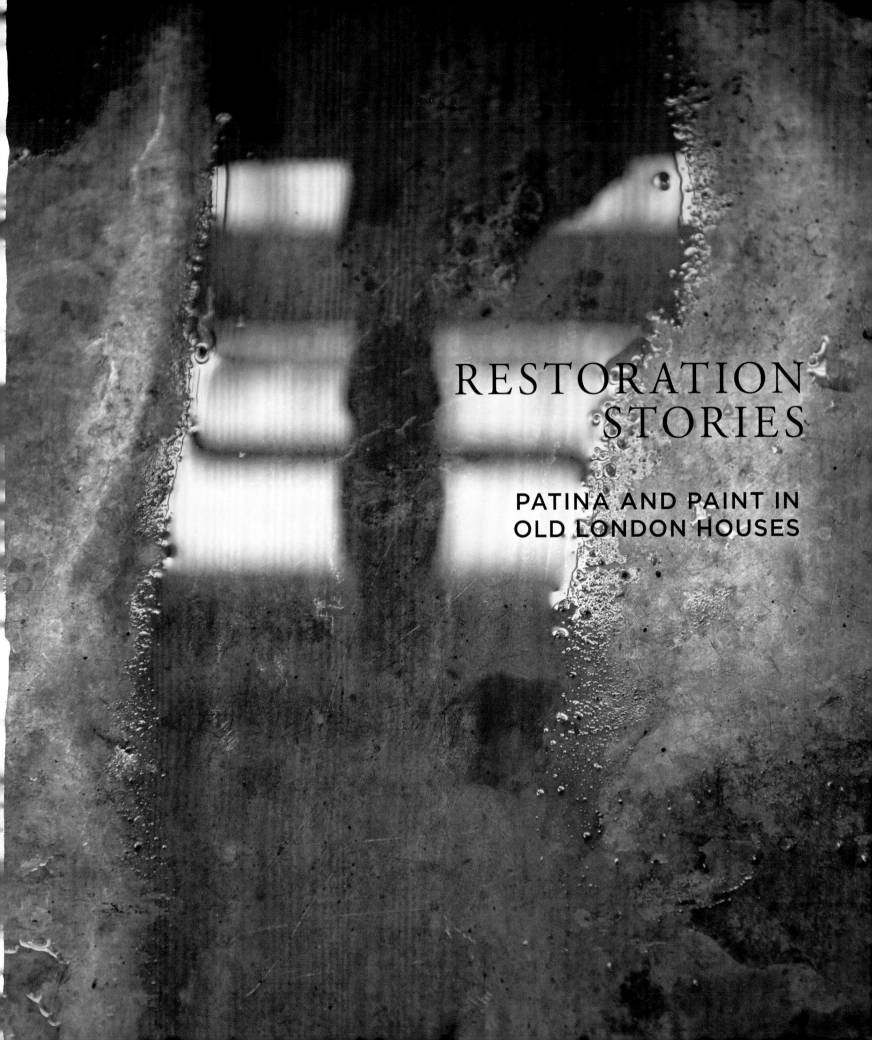

RESTORATION STORIES

PATINA AND PAINT IN OLD LONDON HOUSES

RESTORATION STORIES

PATINA AND PAINT IN OLD LONDON HOUSES

BY PHILIPPA STOCKLEY

PHOTOGRAPHS
CHARLIE HOPKINSON

Pimpernel
Press ltd
www.pimpernelpress.com

CONTENTS

INTRODUCTION

Some of the houses in this book are approaching their 300th birthday. Yet they are still being enjoyed as homes by modern Londoners, who go to work or run a business, fly about in planes – and do not wear wigs or cravats while they do so. Their owners, who come from all walks of life, are proud of the rare beauty of the houses they live in, and find that modern life, equipped with electricity, gas and WiFi, easily coexists with Georgian beauty and practicality. More than that, returning from work to the charm of a judiciously proportioned Georgian house, whose height generally ensures lambent late afternoon light in at least one room – a house that often has a private high-walled back yard (albeit usually quite small) – is a powerful antidote to the stress and speed of the city, as well as an acknowledged privilege. This applies equally to early houses from the 1720s and Regency examples a century later. Yet until quite recently, many of these houses were marked down as uninhabitable and threatened with demolition.

In many respects, this book is a paean to people who put beauty first. From the home of a conservationist active in saving and restoring such old houses and bringing them back into gracious use, to those of a sculptor, a paintmaker, a gardener, a modern-day innkeeper, a Champagne importer and a jeweller – the houses share similarities of temperament, yet each is completely different from the rest. In each case, its beauty speaks for itself.

Each house also serves as a poetic reminder to anyone inclined to make things that won't last or that cannot be recycled and reused, or who continues to argue (thankfully against a slowly but stubbornly rising tide) in favour of demolition and shoddy, deliberately short-term building, that houses made of brick, timber, stone, and lime live, breathe and move; and if left to their own devices will do so for a very long time. They shift and whisper, creak and murmur, particularly on London clay, which itself is inclined to move about, to swell and shrink. It is common for

owners to notice hairline cracks in certain sections of old plaster widen and then narrow or close at about the same time each year; or for a particular door to stick slightly and then release itself according to a repeated seasonal pattern as reliable as the seasons themselves. There is a comforting ship-like quality to the creaking and easing that goes on. A floorboard that creaks, my father told me when I was a child, is a happy floorboard.

Because of this accommodating aspect of their character, like reeds, these houses survive. They will survive the occasional impertinences of beetles, moth, and wetness, for they can be dried out and mended and patched. They are by nature rather gappy and airy, and therefore they provide healthy places to live in that are relatively low in chemicals. Even old lead paint, which is sometimes cited as a dangerous drawback, can, once detected, be attended to if required. When in good condition it needs nothing except to be left in peace, and because of the visual allure of its wonderful, often luminous hues, it isn't hard to spot, which is why many owners of old houses happily coexist with it, understanding how to avoid any potential health risk, enjoying imagining what was going on in the house when it was applied – what the inhabitants looked like, what they wore, how they lived – and the particular colours associated with those far-off inhabitants that may also speak of their wealth (or lack of it), or social aspiration. It is a relief to people who live between walls coloured with traditional oil paints that after a period of disfavour, even large commercial paint manufacturers are once more offering long-lasting, sustainable and eco-friendly oil-based paints as a regular and welcome part of their repertoire.

Meanwhile, another traditional wall finish, limewash, is to a degree antiseptic, antifungal, and prophylactic or at least dissuasive to some infestations, quite aside from being natural, easy to make, easy to apply, and very comely.

Taking a long view forwards, London is fortunate that there are plenty of Victorian houses coming up behind these Georgian ones, some even more tenaciously built. They may not have the same proportions and grace, but they have their own attractions

The original mercury glass of an overmantel mirror with pivoting anthropomorphic brass girandoles creates mystery and invites imaginary glimpses from other times.

and enthusiasts and, besides, over time, tastes change. As long as we take heed to protect *them* from needless or grasping demolition, the next century will also have plenty of equally old houses to astonish and pleasure future generations. And so theoretically, it ought to go on; an experiential renewal through time.

However, if you try to look further forwards than Victorian and Edwardian houses, things get hazier. How many houses, flats, or blocks from the mid-twentieth century onwards are well enough built to last three centuries? How many will we actually want to keep?

There are gentle lessons to learn from the ravishing old houses in this book. Many were built without what we understand today as foundations: rather, with only a few courses of bricks. Their neighbours, their half-basements, and their solid but flexible flagged floors made of three-inch-thick stone often laid directly on sand or dirt hold them up very effectively (along with, now and then, the introduction of some judiciously placed steel). They show that there are economical and renewable ways to make homes entirely compatible with whatever style of life we choose, which, if we build them now, ought to be standing well into the twenty-fourth century.

The houses shown here are not the almost unimaginably grand, aristocratic eighteenth-century houses of, for example, Mayfair, or in parts of the countryside. Architect and mathematician Peter Nicholson's 1823 *The New Practical Builder*[1] (one of many books written after his first, *The Carpenter's New Guide*, which he published in 1792 at the age of twenty-seven) includes a plate of just such a 'first-rate' house. A large, high, deep, three-bay (or four- or five-bay) house, possibly with balconettes to its tall first-floor windows, and with five or six storeys including basements and attic. He did not bother to draw the scaled-down versions: the second-, third- and fourth-rate houses. A little further on, he drew 'a design for a mansion in the castellated style' that is distinctly large and grand and stylistically related to Horace Walpole's Strawberry Hill;[2] as well as, after that, a more restrained, square-plan, detached villa.

Enthusiasm to teach sound building principles can partly be understood as a lingering recollection of the Great Fire of 1665. Certainly, recessing timber windows by a statutory amount, and removing most timber overhangs, made sense.

The desire to spread the design precepts of Palladianism,[3] with its clean lines, generous windows and well-proportioned and well-considered spaces, may also, at first, have been partly reactive; an enjoyment of novelty as well as of elegance. Many pattern books were written with zeal and included copious engraved illustrations. They were mainly aimed at builders and architects and joiners and carpenters, at a time when the distinctions were blurred and

the builder or the carpenter – they often had great practical and frequently overlapping skills – *was* the architect. A relatively early pattern book, and a great success, was *Palladio Londonensis; or, the Art of London Building*, by William Salmon, which went into many editions after its first of 1734. Its attention to geometry in particular would boggle most readers today, but *Palladio Londonensis* was also useful for listing the correct price of every bit of joinery or painting or plumbing or other trade imaginable. Later books were aimed in addition at the house-owning public. George Smith's 1826 *The Cabinet-Maker & Upholsterer's Guide* contained handsome coloured plates at the rear, but was still front-loaded with an indigestible drubbing of geometry. As well as expounding on everything from paints to post beds, with finely drawn examples – and, in the case of paint, an early coloured paint chart – Smith enjoyed occasional digs at other nationalities (and, much more rarely, his own). In a section entitled 'Household Furniture', he writes: 'There are no people of any country whatever that excel the English in the manufacture, the construction, or taste in design as regards the article of cabinet furniture in general . . . The artisans of France are ingenious in their invention, but rarely to be distinguished for their care in construction . . .'

Smith's book aimed to inform the public on the new field of interior decoration. According to architectural and cultural historian and author Steven Parissien,[4] the term 'interior decoration' was first used by Thomas Hope in 1807.[5]

Most houses in the following pages began life as part of an ordinary or fairly ordinary terrace, although there are some distinctly grander ones among them (see pages 80, 90, 140). Time has rendered them all special. Most but not all are listed, generally Grade II – in other words, they are historically important and usually retain at least some original features, but they have in most cases also been adapted by their many inhabitants. Such adaptations can enhance their appeal and interest. The smallest among them were usually 'fourth-rate': often narrow terrace houses of only three or perhaps four floors including attic and basement. For Londoners today who, unlike their forebears, live without servants, it is a perfect size for a couple or a young family. Yet some are a mere fourteen-feet wide. They represent an economical use of land and have a light footprint both actually and metaphorically, while retaining to a surprising degree the charming proportions of their richer cousins. These fourth-rate houses are the town mice, blackened by soot; these are the London sparrows.

One thing that unites many houses featured is that they were saved as a direct result of the work of the Spitalfields Trust, one of the most successful of all building preservation trusts, certainly responsible for saving important parts of historic

Spitalfields in East London, an area now increasingly viewed as not only a valuable asset to Britain, but also a *plein air* museum. Yet when the Trust began in 1977, it was as an almost impromptu, outraged response to the imminent demolition of early eighteenth-century houses in the heart of Spitalfields that year. Indeed, the group only resorted to direct action because demolition had begun on one particular house. Its members then consolidated into a charitable trust.

Among that group of young and ardent house-lovers were author Dan Cruickshank and architectural historians Colin Amery and Mark Girouard. Their vigorous defence, by squatting in a house at which the wrecking ball had already taken a swipe, led not only to the foundation of the Trust but also, over time, to the preservation of some of the most exquisite historic streets in London – and, it is true to say, the world. After its inception, the Trust went on to preserve and restore for reuse and habitation, rather than for speculation and profit, many buildings in London and beyond, and it is still at work today. Indeed, eagle-eyed readers will spot the inclusion of a wild card – a Tudor gatehouse on the Isle of Sheppey, in the Thames estuary. Admittedly not quite in London, it has been included not only because it is unique, and King Henry VIII stayed there, but also because it too was saved by the Spitalfields Trust when there appeared no hope. And so it has been awarded honorary status.

It is almost impossible to believe that the houses we see as so delightful and covetable – in streets that delight millions internationally when they appear as settings for films – were in the mid-twentieth century considered worthless. They had been allowed to decay into a desperately poor state of repair; for those keen to grab and redevelop the land they stood on, this was an easy – not to say facile – argument to make.

For those less familiar with these gracious monuments to daily life, this book hopes to offer a glimpse into a world that is very real, very lovely, very congenial; and whose continuation down the centuries lies in the hearts – and also the hands – of every single one of us.

Philippa Stockley, Whitechapel, London, September 2018

1 Peter Nicholson, *The New Practical Builder and Workman's Companion*, 1823.
2 Novelist Horace Walpole (1717–1797), third son of Britain's first Prime Minister, Sir Robert Walpole, built Strawberry Hill House in Gothic Revival style after buying a site near the Thames in Twickenham in 1747. The villa is open to the public.
3 The term refers to the style of sixteenth-century Italian architect Andrea Palladio (1508–1580). Admired by many eighteenth-century British architects, often after observing it on a Grand Tour, it was reinterpreted in Britain.
4 Steven Parissien, *Interiors: The Home Since 1700*, Laurence King Publishing, 2008, p. 90.
5 Thomas Hope, *Household Furniture and Interior Decoration*, Longman, Hurst, Rees & Orme, 1807. Hope (1769–1831), was a wealthy Dutch-born collector, designer and design-reformer whose work and writings helped shape and define Regency style.

This hall's narrow stair, economically placed to one side, nevertheless invites one up. Signs from the past include the marks left by an oilcloth stair-runner and the slender turned pad of the mahogany handrail, now painted.

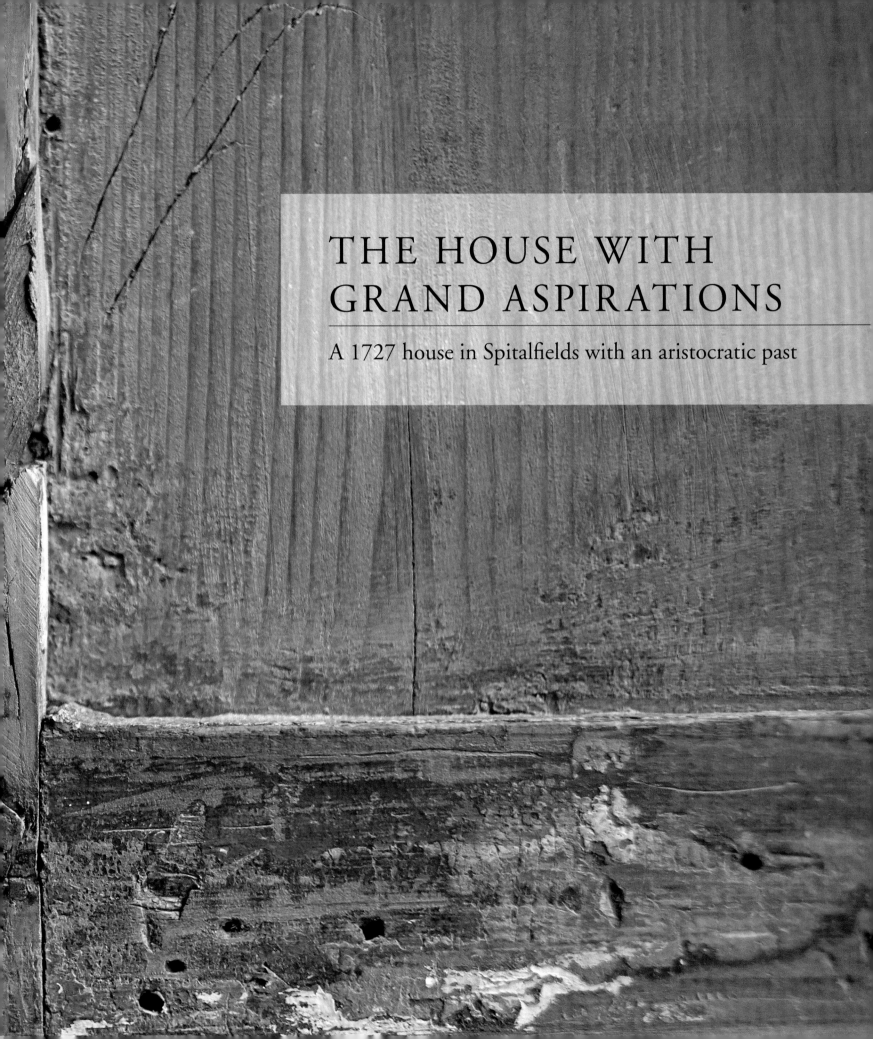

THE HOUSE WITH GRAND ASPIRATIONS

A 1727 house in Spitalfields with an aristocratic past

For a few years on and off in the early 1970s, this four-bay, five-storey, elegantly stuccoed house, built around or soon after 1727,[1] was lived in by a German princess who had become a Guinness by her first marriage. Two hundred and fifty years after its construction, at the turn of the seventies, the striking, unconventional, mini-skirt-wearing, recently separated Mariga Guinness, born in 1932 as Marie-Gabrielle von Urach, bought the house. Not long after this, in 1976, a group of passionate intellectuals and conservationists who shortly afterwards formed the Spitalfields Trust hurled themselves at saving other old nearby houses from demolition by squatting in them.[2] The socialite Mariga helped smooth her new friends' path by inviting politicians and property developers to the glorious parties she held in the house, where she installed a well-equipped bar in a very small closet off the first-floor drawing room, with its own diminutive butler's door opening off the stairs. A triumph of

shoehorning ingenuity that owners Barra, a lawyer, and James, a partner in a PR firm, merely modestly upgraded with handsome brass taps and a lick of sultry dark blue paint, the pint-sized butler's pantry is any drinker's dream room. According to Barra, The Rolling Stones or The Chieftains might play in Mariga's yard, the sound presumably ricocheting off the old bricks. Just as today the sound of bells from Hawksmoor's nearby Christ Church[3] ricochets off a very tall glass skyscraper and rebounds delightfully into a bedroom in the former steeply eaved garret.

Elegant campaigning was a perfect fit for Mariga, for among her several pedigrees she had another: in 1958, she and her first husband, Desmond Guinness, had established the Irish Georgian Society, to save, restore and celebrate Irish Georgian buildings.

Today, the house's sense of innate superiority can still be felt. You see it at once in the shell and Greek key patterns deftly worked into the exterior stucco, which itself hints at the social

Plain deal battens bear numerous nail-holes that would have held a base fabric such as hessian or linen, on to which a surface fabic, probably silk, was neatly pinned and edged.

OPPOSITE Much of historic Spitalfields is characterized by the warm, sober, darkish red brick, with which its terrace houses were fronted. Around 1726, when this house was built, it was not usual in this area to use stucco. But in the early nineteenth century the then owners of the house decided to aggrandize it by adding stucco across the front. Further contemporary and stylish embellishments include a quite modest relief of a raised Greek key pattern.

LEFT Socialite and dedicated conservationist Mariga Guinness, who lived here in the early 1970s, was renowned for entertaining. She concealed a tiny (and charming) butler's pantry behind a small door in the drawing room panelling, with an even more delightful narrow plank-and-brace door on to the stairs. Into this hardworking space, possibly once a powder closet, Mariga adroitly shoehorned a butler's sink and shelves for bottles and glasses. Very appropriate – making the best use of every inch of space, often concealed, was a skill developed to a fine art in the eighteenth century. Two doors allow the easy and discreet circulation of the presiding butler.

aspirations of a former Regency owner who covered the brick that was much more commonly left revealed in these parts – even in far larger and grander houses – with this simulacrum of stone. Rising above that, the house carries itself as if its unusually laid out two principal floors, each consisting of a tiny hall leading to one tiny antechamber that leads to a moderately sized reception room (all connected by doors, so that one could in effect dance an old Irish or English dance in a circle through them) gives it airs. According to *The Survey of London* this house was built under a 61-year lease granted by a William Tillard to a William Goswell. It was mortgaged the following year, 1728, to a Shoreditch gingerbread maker.[4] The majority of houses along the same street just had one L-shaped room, for the street was not grand, and as *The Survey* observes with a degree of asperity, in the mid-eighteenth century, several residents along it were sent to court for keeping hogs.

'Many people think that because these houses are old, they must be difficult to live in,' explains Barra, 'but it is the reverse. They were handmade for people *by* people, to a very human scale, with well-proportioned rooms that are made to live in.'

Barra had dreamed of owning the house for a long time before the couple bought it in 2014. When younger, he had rented nearby, and his daily walk to work took him right past it. 'I wondered what it would be like to live there, and dreamed of owning it.' Years passed before the chance arose.

'You either see it or you don't,' he says; 'but once you get the bug for the magic of these houses, you want to preserve it and contribute to it. I often sit and just look at the panelling and the patina. There is a sense of such satisfaction, and of connection to such houses.'

But when the couple bought it, it felt even to them as if the house was losing its soul. Plasterboard and cream paint

obliterated most of the panelled walls, though fortunately they still lurked beneath. In the dining room, a blue silk once nailed to battens on the walls above the dado panelling had been replaced with bobbly cream 'wild' silk. The passage down the side of the house that originally ran to the yard had been incorporated into the living space and was now a dank, poorly lit plasterboarded pantry.

At the end of the hall, the staircase, twisting in a fairly tight spiral around a single vertical spar of Baltic pine, neat pegs still visible, was fundamentally sound, but it and most of the board floors had been varnished, probably in the seventies, and had acquired the loathsome orange cast familiar to everyone who lived through that decade. But it was not all bad: the original internal shutters and their hinges were still there, and many of the door latches and catches. This was a happy discovery. Most of the yard was covered over with a simple glazed structure, in

LEFT In the kitchen, the hand-painted rims of salt-glazed hand-thrown bowls echo the bead on the scraped-back deal panels behind, which still bear traces of a pretty lead-based green.

CENTRE When restoring an eighteenth-century house – or any historic house – it is vital to conserve original details. Here, handmade 'H' hinges add veracity and charm to a cupboard in the master bedroom.

RIGHT Nothing can match the patina and subtle variation of paint abraded and faded over time. The slight colour variations in old lead paint are partly due to the varied grind and size of the pigment particles in its composition, which refract light in different ways. In some lights, the paint seems to dance and glitter. Here, on bead-and-butt finely cut by hand, dried and shifted, paint-layered and holding an iron key on a nail, it invites contemplation.

which there was a kitchen. Given that it was sound and well lit, they decided just to repair it.

They removed the plasterboard throughout, and took down the cream silk in the dining room. They discovered that this intimate square room's back wall had been bodged together with an old window and other repurposed bits and pieces; an eighteenth- and nineteenth-century habit of scrupulous reuse far more common than is always realized today. The pair also repaired the chimney breast panelling and added a 1720s fire surround. Having removed the silk and the old canvas on which it was mounted, they left one scarred pine wall exposed, with all its nail-holes, scratches and marks. Scarred, pricked, and now darkened simply through the passage of time, the exposed wood is very attractive.

The beautiful arched china alcove to the left-hand side of the fireplace, which would always have been used for display, was in good condition. To populate it, Barra bought a partial Coalport dining service for just £75 on eBay. It arrived wrapped in blankets, with several numbered notebooks tucked inside the soup tureen. In them, a neat hand meticulously describes dinner-party guests and menus in fountain pen. At one dinner from 1970, *potage parmentier, escalopes de veau à la crème* and a lemon sorbet were served.

Throughout the house, walls and panelling were repaired or reconstructed where needed by the local joiner. In the kitchen and pantry the flags were lifted and re-laid with lime pointing, and new bespoke glazed hardwood doors to the small yard were installed.

All the faded varnish was hand-scraped from the stairs and the floorboards, which were then patched and scrubbed, before being waxed with beeswax polish. Bit by bit, the house re-emerged.

But some twentieth-century additions added such charm that they were left. Mariga Guinness had, says Barra, 'hacked a small window into the panelled wall between her bathroom and the hall'. They kept this little oblong window with its two vertical glazing bars, just as they kept her butler's pantry. But the nasty downstairs pantry, once it was taken back to the original walls, which they replastered using lime, makes a fine flagged cloakroom lit by a carriage lamp; and even though it is unlikely ever to have housed a sedan chair kept ready to whisk a mistress or a master off to an assignment in town at any time of day or night, it is tempting to imagine the possibility.

TOP This partial Coalport dinner service, bought online, arrived in the post with the pieces, including this soup tureen, wrapped in blankets. The tureen has been used for dinner parties.

ABOVE Several notebooks listing menus and guests of the 1960s and 1970s came with the service.

RIGHT Panelling; faux-painted porphyry on the column holding a bust of Eros; polished, wide floorboards; and a small mahogany hall chair just visible, all contribute drama and gravitas to the hall.

1 *Survey of London: Volume 27, Spitalfields and Mile End New Town*, ed. FHW Sheppard (London: London County Council, 1957), 81-87. *British History Online* http://www.british-history.ac.uk/survey-london/vol27/pp81-87
2 Once formed, the Trust was able to buy and restore these buildings.
3 Nicholas Hawksmoor (1661-1736) was an English architect. In 1711, parliament passed an act to design 50 churches in London, Westminster and the suburbs. Of only twelve ever built, six were designed by Hawksmoor. They include Christ Church, Spitalfields, built 1714-1729.
4 *Survey of London: Volume 27, Spitalfields and Mile End New Town*, ed. FHW Sheppard (London: London County Council, 1957), 81-87. *British History Online* http://www.british-history.ac.uk/survey-london/vol27/pp81-87

LEFT Bust of Eros looking into the blue dining room to keep an eye on things: perhaps to make sure that love is not forgotten (or that the George II mahogany drop-leaf dining table is sufficiently polished?). This Eros, a Victorian copy of a Greek original, came from a castle on the Isle of Wight. The chips and knocks on his pedestal enhance his beauty.

TOP RIGHT In a vaulted side passage that now stores wine, a glazed hanging carriage lamp gives beautiful light and varied shadow.

BOTTOM RIGHT Painting the door the same colour as the dado panelling contributes to character. Undercoat has been cleverly used to create the dead flat blue, deep and soft.

ABOVE An elegant collection of old and new plaster casts and Old Master drawings collected over time, set above a sofa covered in loose linen, gives elegance to this small retiring room off the drawing room. The mixture includes a circular framed wax cast of a bust of Marie Antoinette; nineteenth-century copies of fragments of the frieze from the Acropolis; plaster casts by modern master Peter Hone; and a drawing attributed to seventeenth-century French artist Antoine Coypel. The collection is balanced rhythmically between the vertical muntins of the panelling.

RIGHT There is still much aesthetic pleasure, as well as comfort, to be had from this monumental eighteenth-century wingback chair covered in costly salmon-pink silk velvet, its surface silvered by the sun. Where the side has been torn loose one sees the original bright colour, the strong linen warp threads that take the silk weft, the quite basic deal structure and the webbing.

FAR LEFT Mariga Guinness cut a horizontal hole in the panels between her bathroom and the landing and had it glazed with two vertical glazing bars. The technique of borrowed light is an old one. The window is not only a historic memento, but gives an otherwise dark room light.

LEFT A French freestanding copper slipper bath that would once have been filled by a maid lugging hot water from the range, carefully plumbed into the corner of the attic bedroom. The standing brass mixer tap comes from a reclamation yard. Although baths were often lined with linen before use, copper is warm to the skin.

ABOVE A romantic bedroom set economically under sharply angled eaves clad in painted pine enjoys light from both sides. And the sound of the bells of nearby Christ Church bounces off the first of the glass skyscrapers built on the fringe of Spitalfields and the City, straight through the window – an unexpected development that Hawksmoor might have enjoyed.

OPPOSITE Views from one room to another are softly framed by the uneven edges of often-painted wood. The master bedroom, seen from the hall, is kept light and plain with neutral tinted paints and sparse furnishings, a good setting for a large fine-spindled English Windsor, or Thames Valley, chair.

BELOW LEFT A sixteenth-century carved oak chest displays three eighteenth-century blue-and-white majolica bowls from Granada in Spain. Panels from a sixteenth-century Low Countries triptych hang above.

BELOW RIGHT The master bedroom evokes monastic austerity, an effect offset by beautiful light. This calm space, palely scented with beeswax-polished wood, with no modern distractions, provides an ideal retreat.

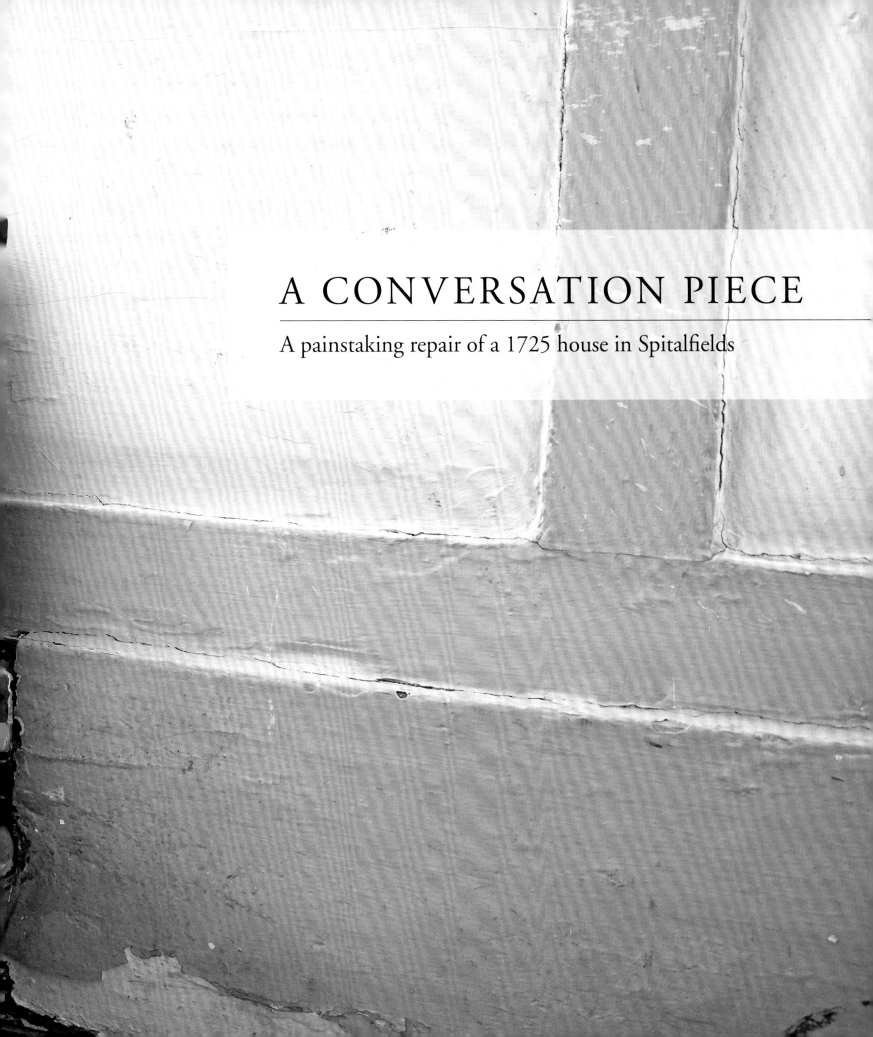

A CONVERSATION PIECE

A painstaking repair of a 1725 house in Spitalfields

'I love conversation pieces, and I suppose that's what I'm trying to create,' says barrister Phillip Lucas. Submerged in an early eighteenth-century wing-back armchair in a corner of his south drawing room, he sits between two portraits and opposite a conversation piece high on the wall beside the chimney breast.

The room forms the conclusion of an enfilade of three panelled rooms, one pint-size, on the first floor of his Spitalfields house, which was probably built between 1724 and 1725. This square, high-ceilinged principal room effortlessly holds an extraordinary range of beautiful things: walnut chairs and a pedestal table ideal for an intimate supper before a roaring fire; side tables, paintings, porcelain; a very old coffee pot. An old overmantel mirror with its original smoky mercury glass faintly reflects a larger mirror on the other side: mirrors that one always feels might without warning reflect someone else's face entirely.

His desk is here, too, somehow not incongruous despite its computer and modern appurtenances.

The drawing room is on the southern flank of a house that is wide but only one room deep – oddly reminiscent of the boxy, broad-panniered form of the skirts of an eighteenth-century court dress. Light shifts across and warms the original quite plain panelling, which Phillip painted a sludge 'holding colour' soon after buying the house in 2009. One day, he says, he will carefully scrape the paint layers back by hand in search of the original colour. It is a patient, slow process that he admits might take ten years to get around to completing in the entire five-storey house. 'I like browny greens and greeny browns, the sort of colours you see in attics. They make a perfect foil for paintings and furniture.' That is definitely true of this indeterminate group of colours loosely and variously known as duns, drabs,

and sludges. Partly because of its eloquently quiet background, and despite the number of things it contains, the luminous room feels both serene and all of a piece.

'I've always been a collector of things – for as long as I can remember,' Phillip says. A childhood interest in Smurfs and *Star Wars* soon transmogrified into George II[1] furniture. Even as a schoolboy in Winchester, his pocket money went on Georgian tea caddies and writing slopes, then on sofas. 'There's only so far you can go with tea caddies,' he observes, drily. By the time he was at university, he couldn't resist dawn raids on antiques markets and fairs, selling his finds as a fledgling dealer.

'I learned the hard way, by handling things, by going to museums. There's no substitute for handling things, though it can be fun to make mistakes.' Over those years his taste changed from Regency to neoclassicism, settling at last on the period from 1690 to 1730.

PREVIOUS PAGES Original lead paint, chipped and buffeted over the centuries, the skirts picked out in a darker tone, sets off the staircase. A fireback waits to find a resting place, as do reclaimed floorboards. Any owner of an old house carefully marshals leftover bits of board for future reuse.

OPPOSITE This probably started as a respectable weaver's house, sparingly furnished with smart metropolitan oak and walnut furniture – 'not grand, and not William Kent'. The south drawing room is appointed with furniture and paintings from the owner's favourite period, 1690–1730.

ABOVE In the north drawing room, sinuous but solid walnut chairs gather round a tea table. The tight-grained walnut has an almost liquid appearance. Tricorn hat boxes are stacked on another table, and beyond is a small powder chamber, or cabinet.

His love of Georgian architecture was kindled by a school visit to No.1, Royal Crescent, Bath.[2] Once in London, he gravitated, architectural gazetteer in hand, towards Spitalfields, where a visit to Dennis Severs's house[3] was 'a powerful experience. It felt as if I had arrived.' He had lived in several Georgian houses when friends alerted him to an office building for sale in Spitalfields, once a dwelling house, but long occupied by an investment company. Aesthetically, nothing appeared to have been done to the building for decades. A synthetic green, floral, nylon carpet laid throughout had coffee trails running from room to room and puddling around the doors; but at least the rooms still had their original configuration – although Phillip would discover that most of the floorboards were damaged, some joists had been all but sawn through, and ugly heating pipes and ducts ran amok.

The wide basement, once probably divided into a wet and a dry kitchen, had been thoroughly meddled with. One side had been converted to an office kitchen with Mexican tiles and peeling melamine. All the original shutters and a dresser had gone. There was 'a boiler that belched carbon monoxide, and a cooker called a Falcon Dominator'. The other side had been divided with breeze blocks into seven urinals and one ladies' toilet; it also held two enormous fire safes, which had to be winched out with a block and tackle. The windows were blocked.

RIGHT A beautiful early eighteenth-century Carrara marble fire surround, bought for the house, beneath a gilded mercury overmantel mirror, with a painting by a follower of Canaletto above. These mirrors add entrancing, mysterious light, but only if their magical glass is intact.

OPPOSITE, LEFT This house was full of original material, but all the secondary leaves had been removed from the internal window shutters, which had been nailed back. A few of the eighteenth-century shutter hinges, including this one, were being used to hang a door. Exact copies were diligently handmade to restore the shutters.

OPPOSITE, RIGHT All the internal shutters had to be gently released from the wall, and new secondary leaves were made using reclaimed eighteenth-century pine. Once that was done, they were joined together with handmade etched H-hinges and painted in a slub colour.

Undeterred, Phillip set to with a sledge hammer, demolishing the breeze blocks, reopening windows, and stripping the house of intolerable excrescences. Remarkably, when the offices were created in the 1970s, one of the founders of the Spitalfields Trust, Dan Cruickshank, had saved and stored the basement's discarded internal shutters and dresser, which in due course he returned to their rightful home and its new owner.

The first and second floors are each divided into an enfilade of two square-ish drawing rooms, one to each side of the landing. The northern room leads to a small powder room, or closet. Entirely filling the second-floor closet directly above, a monstrous automated steel filing system 'that lifted files out and handed them to you' had to be cut out with a sabre saw. 'The whole house was a Gordian knot,' Phillip says.

But for a person who had collected boxes of old hinges and architectural elements since his teens, this was not an insurmountable challenge. Shockingly, all the secondary shutters had been removed and the shutters nailed back, but one chamber door had been artfully if precariously hung on shutter hinges; and one cupboard still had its original foliate H hinges. Phillip took careful stock, then had all the missing hinges copied bespoke in Westport, USA, with hand-bevelled edges and engraved lines. Such poetic details make an enormous difference.

LEFT, TOP & BOTTOM
The central staircase is unusually set forward about a foot from the back wall of the house. Since brick walls offer support, this is fairly innovative. When the house was acquired the staircase was dark, but investigation revealed a blocked roof light at the top, designed to throw light down through the centre, behind the balustrades and landings. When reopened and restored it let limpid light through the core of the building, reaching every part except the basement.

He repaired damaged floorboards with reclaimed Baltic pine from the same period. A carpenter worked on site for almost two years, patching and replacing.

This house has an unusual and attractive staircase, set in about a foot from the back wall, which makes its construction and support complex. The vertical lightwell behind it appears to have been designed to allows softly filtering light from a blocked-up light at the top, which Phillip uncovered and repaired. And the light is intriguing and luminous, not only on the stair and landings, but in the connecting rooms on the principal floor, which have great charm and character, and appear to glance at each other sideways as one passes between. There is something about a glimpsed or half-glimpsed room that is both profoundly rewarding and sometimes unsettling.

The basement, in which little had been left unmolested, was carefully reflagged, its walls replastered with lime, and the missing sections of its tongue-and-groove ceiling carefully reinstated using old wood. With their low ceilings and daylight from restored windows, the kitchen and scullery have strong character, but as one would expect, it is the upper rooms that have true grace.

Here, peopled by the almost liquid gleam of polished walnut, by genial if formal portraits, and by a satisfying muddle of lovely things, there is a sense of life lost and life gained. 'If you take an eighteenth-century room, any eighteenth-century furniture will fit into it. Even just a few things will bring it back to life. I like splits and repairs in panels and I like teapots with mended handles, or porcelain bowls with staples. I think perhaps they understand that better in America.

'It is all about atmosphere, character and charm, and about not trying to make things what they are not. I like honest damage and honest repairs. I like . . . truthfulness; it is a good word to use.

'I've tried to get back to the truth of the building, in order to make a sequence of eighteenth-century rooms that are as powerfully evocative as I can make them. I like putting pieces of furniture back where they belong, where they fit and glow. Colour and patination are so important with furniture: they add to the character of the object. And I collect things – such as tobacco boxes – which have personal inscriptions.

'I don't see the point of eliminating signs of life. It is the human aspect that appeals to me.'

ABOVE Patch-tests of colour on the neutral backdrop of an olive-drab paint used on this simply panelled 1726 door show what a good foil such earth-based drabs make.

1 George II (1683–1760), reigned as King of Great Britain 1727–1760. The Georgian period is defined by four successive kings called George: George I (reigned 1714–1727); George II; George III (reigned 1760–1801 as King of Great Britain and 1801–1820 as King of the United Kingdom), and George IV (reigned 1820–1830). 1811–1820 was the Regency period, when George III was considered unable to rule and his son, later George IV, ruled as Prince Regent.
2 A museum set in the end house of the Royal Crescent in Bath, a crescent of thirty terrace houses designed by John Wood the Younger and built 1767–1774.
3 Dennis Severs's house: a house museum at 18 Folgate Street, London, E1, dating from 1724.

LEFT An enfilade of rooms should have some visual links. Good diffuse light on the first-floor landing makes it the perfect place to try out paint tones (mixed from combinations of earth pigments from red oxide to raw umber to yellow ochre) and judge the effect against the following room.

OPPOSITE, TOP There is delight in the various holes and fixings and patches and alterations in colour that have been made all over the house – in this example, to a door. In previous ages, more frugal (and sometimes more intelligent?) than ours, doors were often patched, rehung, or flipped from one side of the case to the other.

OPPOSITE, BOTTOM On the other side of the same door is a very pretty rim-lock with its delicate eighteenth-century handle, in a pattern still being made today.

LEFT A Portuguese terracotta bust of a late seventeenth- or early eighteenth-century young gentleman, poetically dressed. On one side, a tress of his wig has been tied with a fine ribbon as a romantic gesture, possibly a pledge, and his cravat is distinctly raffish. In the seventeenth and eighteenth centuries men could make bold statements through dress. This rake clearly had strong views on how he wanted to be immortalized. Recently unpacked, the bust waits to find its place in the house.

BELOW The corner of the north drawing room holds a charming group comprising an appealing 1722 portrait of a young man, Edward Allen, in a grey velvet coat, two giltwood Corinthian capitals, and a Roman marble torso, all set off by the honest practicality of oak tricorn boxes, used for travelling or storage.

RIGHT Decorative mouldings such as these might be carved as samples for an element of a cornice or door case or piece of furniture. Today, along with any reclaimed leftover sections, they are lovely things to collect, display, make drawings from, or as a reminder of lost practical skills and artistry.

BELOW Three sections of marble frieze create a dynamic still life, back-lit on a window seat: two fragments from an eighteenth-century frieze frame a metaphorical fragment – of Age admiring Beauty – from a seventeenth-century frieze. Translucent marble such as Carrara changes in different lights.

LEFT An elegant dressing glass supported on a box benignly reflects several wigs on stands nearby, and itself rests on a small writing desk with a pretty knee scoop. The mirror is surrounded by toilet appurtenances, which include a tortoiseshell-mounted clothes brush, two pomanders, an ivory shoehorn and a small Delft tulip vase.

RIGHT Phillip says that eighteenth-century furniture will sit well in any eighteenth-century room. The same is true of smaller items. In the small chamber, the top and extended flap of a writing bureau is used as a display stand for three related *famille verte* vases, wine glasses, and other decorative pieces.

RIGHT A double copper sink in the basement kitchen, served by brass taps, with copper tankards on the windowsill, gleams in the soft light filtering in. It is difficult to imagine that this basement was previously clumsily divided up into toilets, with all the windows blocked up.

BELOW Little was left in the kitchen except some original tongue-and-groove on the ceiling. It was repaired using recycled eighteenth-century wood to copy and replace missing parts. Flagstones, a fire, country oak furniture – including a massive oak table from the former Church Farmhouse Museum in Hendon, London – bring the room alive.

OPPOSITE Once the ceiling was repaired, still with its original, massy oak beam running from side to side, the kitchen was limewashed. A mounting block makes attractive steps up to the dwarf door to the enclosed back yard.

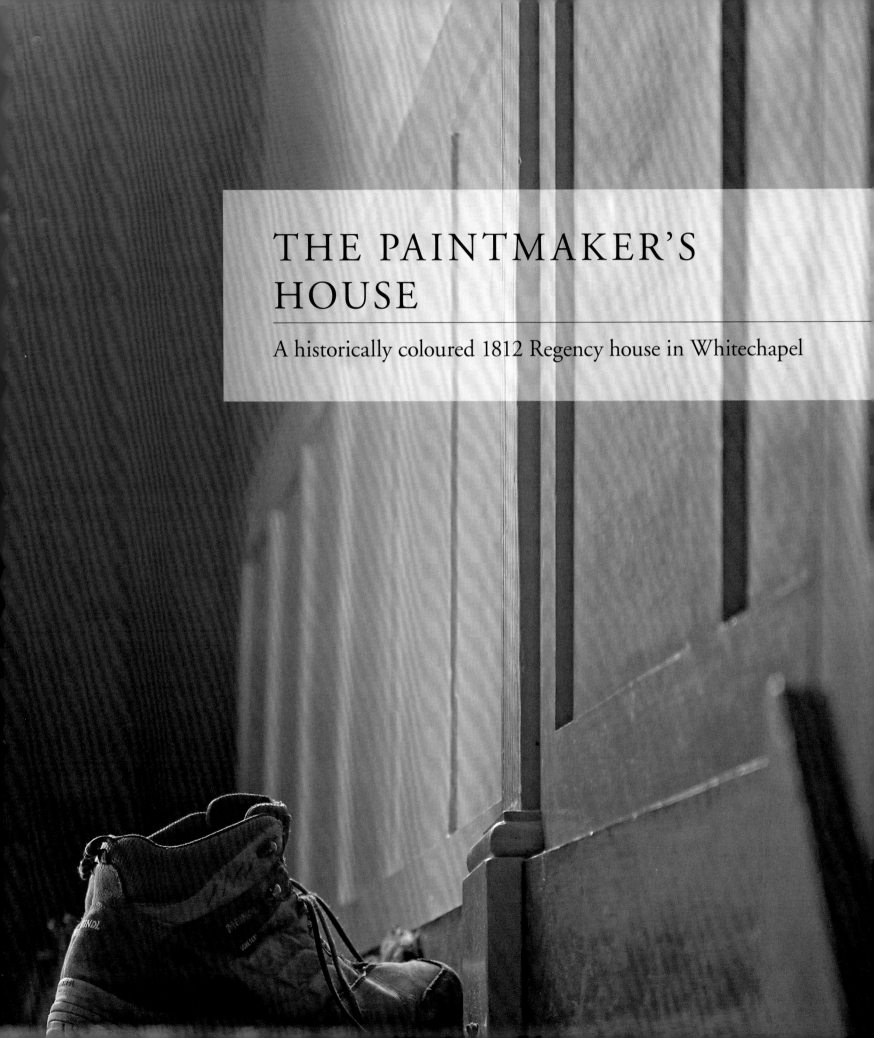

THE PAINTMAKER'S HOUSE

A historically coloured 1812 Regency house in Whitechapel

A deep blue-green: underwater, velvety, almost ominous until sunlight through the front-door fanlight flames it peacock. The unusual colour of one side of the narrow hall in paint specialist Pedro Da Costa Felgueiras's Whitechapel house presages the rest. For colour is the most noticeable thing here. Not for being strident or garish, but because it is muted, subtle, sometimes sombre, and brought to dancing life by sudden light through panes of watery Crown glass.

With its large-flagged basement kitchen with roaring fire and Windsor chairs; its rooms panelled, half-panelled and lightly corniced; its Regency grates, one stamped Coalbrookdale,[1] framed by painted fire surrounds; its charming bathrooms with casual lead splashbacks – even to the bath – it is hard to recognize the terminally neglected fourth-rate terrace house, built around 1812, which narrowly escaped demolition in 2006. For it was one of the same group as Tim Whittaker's house (see page 132).

Rebuilding took two years, during which time there were no front steps, so Pedro hopped up into the front door, until a traditional stonemason cut steps to a late Georgian pattern that Pedro sketched from a nearby Regency house. 'I don't like temporary things,' he shrugs. That stonemason is now gone, as is the man who cast the railings. Many such skills are lost. Having made something habitable, Pedro took a further five years – between his paint conservation and restoration work at, for example, Horace Walpole's masterpiece, Strawberry Hill House – to paint and limewash, room by room, mixing all the colours himself.

In winter 2006, when he first saw his future home, the spine wall was exposed, all plaster gone; the narrow stairs only ran from raised-ground to first floor, and the basement was 'knee-deep in rubbish'. He created a formal garden laid out between high, warm-tinted garden walls of reclaimed brick with brushed lime-mortar, which bear neatly espaliered apple and pear trees. At the end, a delightful folly of a shed with pantile roof and horticultural lapped glass between vertical glazing bars is protected with red-oxide paint. 'I made the shed with leftovers.' But when he bought the house there was just a car park, and a car or truck had knocked the back corner of the house off. Decades earlier, a flat felt roof had been installed, resulting in water damage.

PREVIOUS PAGES Intense blue verditer applied on sheets of paper above ochre-coloured half-panelling adds drama to a narrow hall.

BELOW & OPPOSITE At the far end of the formal walled garden laid to espaliered fruit trees and gravel walks is the garden shed. Built from leftover bricks and handmade clay roof tiles, it is a useful place for potting and storage. The windows of lapped horticultural glass between vertical astragals in traditional style are painted with red-oxide paint made from iron oxide, famously long-wearing outside, even in low temperatures. The same colour graces the reclaimed Regency door. Inside, old wooden crates, simple furniture and a Portuguese ceramic dish hold everything a gardener needs, while coloured bottles glow like large boiled sweets on the windowsill.

BELOW The 'Grand Tour' dining room has a refined fireplace surround with carved wood dentil frieze beneath the mantel and walls painted an elegant pale lilac-pink. A Portuguese majolica snake coils lazily on the square Georgian drop-leaf dining table, while Rita, a young German shorthair pointer, looks out of the window in the vain hope of passing rabbits.

OPPOSITE Even in small Regency houses, the long-established tradition of conjoined front and back rooms with doors that could be opened or closed continued. Here the doors had already been removed. The back room, with light from two sides, is a more informal space in which to sit by the fire, listen to old records, or read.

Keeping Dennis Severs's house, as well as neighbouring Regency houses, in mind, and aware of how relatively ordinary his house once was, Pedro set to with a joiner and carpenter to put things back, to repair, recut, reinstall, and reimagine.

Colour performs the final trick here, pulls the curtain aside to reveal . . . what? A whiff of 1812, perhaps. In the kitchen, limewash for the walls, which dries to a dazzling white. 'Twenty or thirty coats,' he says. For the cupboards beside the hearths he mixed what he calls 'Oxford yellow' – an ochre-ish colour, pragmatic and easy on the eye.

The doors – almost all remade, and rare knobs and fasteners found – are painted in Caput Mortuum. A door in this delicious dark-brown colour, which Pedro says was popular in the

nineteenth century, resembles a bar of 90 per cent chocolate, so deep and warm a brown it is. He also used it on the narrow skirts and the stair risers; practical Georgian touches for the places exposed to most dirt and wear. Now quite rare (Mayer[2] calls it obsolete), the pigment is having a modest revival. It is made from haematite, a violet-ish iron-oxide (Fe_2O_3). A similar colour was once made from ground-up mummies and known as Mummy or Egyptian brown.

The first-floor 'Grand Tour' dining room is in an evanescent lavender-pink that perfectly sets off plaster casts, two painted wood Regency pilasters and framed engravings of Rome. Pedro calls it Ecclesiastical Purple, mixed from cochineal and blue verditer in white. The once widely used blue pigment is a copper carbonate achieved through a fairly complex process. It is the chemical equivalent of azurite. Pedro says it was the first imitation of costly ultramarine (made from lapis lazuli), and fashionable around 1750 and on into the nineteenth century. It was certainly used in the seventeenth century, when it was made using an even more complex technique.[3]

The original partition is painted in a modern approximation of lead white. Since it is almost impossible to recreate lead's almost saturnine off-white, Pedro added small amounts of raw umber and other pigments to produce an alternative white.

And, where we first came in, the peacock hall. Here, he laid down the largest size of paper available in 1812, called elephant – near A1 to a modern eye. On top went distemper, made with rabbit-skin glue, pigment and chalk, for blue verditer goes translucent in oil.

On the colours go, some unusual, some not, up the house. A gorgeous greenish grey in the master bedroom at the top, which with its glazed partition to the bathroom resembles a weavers' loft, was mixed with impenetrably dark spinel black (a manganese-iron oxide); while the panelling of the landing bathroom is done in indigo 'left over from painting Gilbert and George's house'. [4]

Pedro was raised in old Lisbon: a place he nicely describes as giving the impression of being a century behind. When he was a child, his father went to collect freshly milked milk each morning. He grew up surrounded by faded limewash on old buildings; absorbed the unmistakeable look and variations of hand-mixed paint finishes as they mellow; absorbed the look, too, of Portuguese crafts, including faience, terracotta, porcelain and tiles.

After going to Lisbon art college, in 1990 he moved to London and worked with lacquer – a slow finish built up layer by layer. He was living in architect Denys Lasdun's East London Brutalist

block, Keeling House,[5] when he was told of the Spitalfields Trust's ambitious project to restore a group of Regency houses threatened with demolition, and encouraged to join the group and to buy and restore one in association with the Trust.

Because he has also worked since then in such places as Strawberry Hill, Pedro says he is associated with eighteenth-century houses. But things aren't quite so simple: 'People think that because I live in a Georgian house I only like old houses, but no: I like Georgian houses because they are so well designed and proportioned; because they represent the Enlightenment, when art and science and rationality and intellect became dominant. I like things because of the quality of their design, whether old or new.' This truth is borne out by many modern touches in

BELOW LEFT The original stairs leading down from the attic loft afford a pleasing view of the bathroom which has been built In the extension on the back. An originally small and quite low attic room was built up to create something like a weavers' loft, with good head-height and stairs remade from the original ones, nothing wasted.

BELOW RIGHT A chair, carefully placed, offers a simple and effective way to decorate a difficult area. Set against the bedroom wall, this informal Regency chair with prettily turned spindles can also do duty to hold clothes or books.

his house, from mid-twentieth-century furniture, to lamps, to a record collection that rolls from Josephine Baker to Benjamin Britten; to modern Portuguese ceramics done with traditional techniques, which gleam and glisten all around the house.

For Pedro, Eileen Gray[6] put it perfectly: 'She became a modernist architect because she was brought up in a Georgian house in Ireland that she described as "a beautifully proportioned white cube with embellishments".'

Contemplating the shimmer of the blue-green of the hall wall and the time and effort it took to achieve, he adds: 'I want to do the most authentic paint, and finish. I don't mind how long it takes, or whether it is complicated or not.'

1 Coalbrookdale in Shropshire was renowned for decorative ironwork.

2 Ralph Mayer, *The Artist's Handbook of Materials and Techniques*, Faber & Faber, 1987.

3 Ian C. Bristow, *Interior House-Painting Colours and Technology 1615–1840*, published for the Paul Mellon Centre for Studies in British Art by Yale University Press, 1996.

4 Gilbert and George: a world-famous London-based artistic duo composed of Gilbert Prousch, born 1943, and George Passmore, born 1942. They met in 1967 at St Martin's School of Art (now Central St Martin's) and have worked together since on monumental photography-based works which, while secular, often bear a visual similarity to stained glass.

5 Sir Denys Lasdun, architect, 1914–2001. His key London Brutalist concrete buildings include Keeling House in Bethnal Green, completed 1957, and the National Theatre on the South Bank, completed in 1976.

6 Modernist architect Eileen Gray (1878–1976) learned Japanese lacquer techniques in Paris and became a pioneering architect and furniture designer.

BELOW LEFT The understated utility of a modern metal light fitting, such as this bulb on a once-again-fashionable traditional twisted flex, complements the Georgian setting.

BELOW RIGHT This modern post bed harks back to country beds of earlier centuries, often made equally simply. Without cumbersome hangings, such a bed creates drama and glamour, while not being at all stuffy or blocking light. Welsh blankets woven in organic colours, a glazed coloured engraving of the goddess Clytie on the back wall, and a lamp from a vintage shop complete the look.

OPPOSITE Lapped sheet lead makes an unusual splashback and shower enclosure for an ordinary steel bath set in the corner. Left to its own devices the lead will patinate attractively, so there is no need to clean it, although it can be rinsed down from time to time. As lead is heavy, it is essential to fix it well. (Such a splashback is only suitable for adult use and where lead's potential toxicity is understood. A similar effect could be achieved with non-toxic zinc sheet.)

ABOVE LEFT Interior glazing for the small new bathroom off the bedroom is handsome as well as practical in terms of bringing in borrowed light.

ABOVE RIGHT A charming arrangement of a generous shelf for bottles and bathroom effects; pine wooden panelling painted an ambient colour; a small lead offcut from lead flashing as a splashback; reclaimed brass bib taps, and a butler's sink.

ALL FLESH IS GRASS

LEFT In this bedroom, a carpenter installed dado panelling, a quite plain timber fire surround appropriate for a bedroom, and, in the alcoves, cupboards carefully copied from examples in the house. They were all then painted a good stone colour with a warm yellowish tone. The Regency grate, bought online, was filthy, but when it was cleaned a mark along the bottom revealed its maker, the famous forge of Coalbrookdale.

RIGHT A plain post bed has been painted a rich yellow ochre colour to harmonize with the panelling and the warm cream walls. Yellow-toned Welsh blankets add inviting comfort. Blinds maximize space, while their red-brown tone adds character.

BELOW LEFT Stacks of glazed Portuguese ceramic bowls and plates, many modern but made using traditional techniques, offer a colourful display inside a cupboard built across an alcove. The Georgians made good use of the deep recesses on either side of a chimney breast. The cupboard was painted in a yellow similar to Naples yellow but made with non-toxic pigments including yellow ochre. Painting the insides a contrasting colour, here a soft blue, makes a pretty effect when the door is open. The mouldings are modest, as befits a kitchen.

BELOW RIGHT An instant still life made from an attractive pile of old books and a dried flower.

BELOW When the owner moved in nothing existed of this practical kitchen. Indeed little remained anywhere in the house except some original panelling and moulding details which could be copied. It took two years to rebuild and reinstate the timber parts of the house, and a further five years to paint it. The kitchen design is spare, with a modern range set in the hearth, which vents naturally up the chimney, and a run of cupboards against the window. Round holes in the cupboard door fronts, as well as being decorative, allow ventilation, and small flat metal knobs give an authentic look. Hefty flagstones were usual in Georgian basements, where they acted as a sort of foundation. The kitchen walls have been limewashed – limewash being a traditional finish made by mixing lime putty and water and applying it in many layers to create a luminous and slightly velvety, slightly chalky surface that is instantly recognizable.

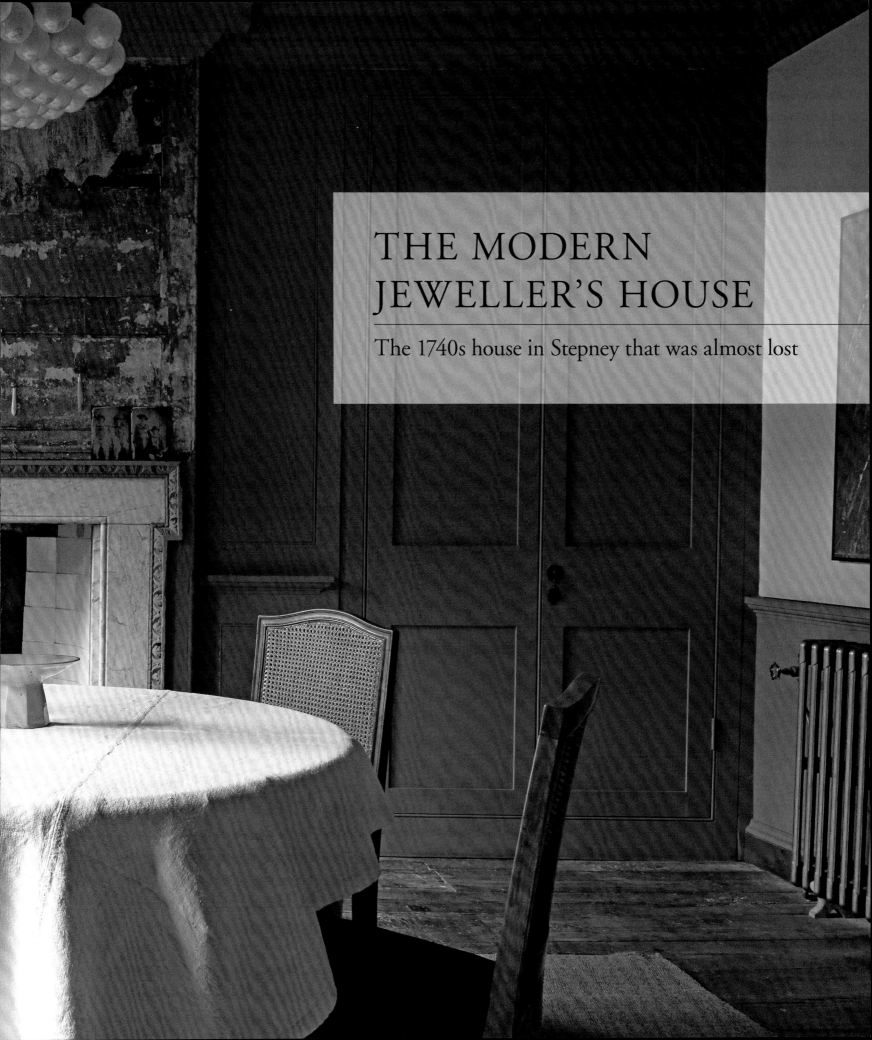

THE MODERN
JEWELLER'S HOUSE

The 1740s house in Stepney that was almost lost

Centuries ago, Mile End Road was an important route between Mile End and Aldgate, once the eastern gate of the old city. But after an elegant start the area declined rapidly, and it is a sad truth that houses in such areas often decline too, or are demolished. At the turn of the twenty-first century, that was the impending fate of an imposing pair of eighteenth-century Mile End dwellings.

An account[1] by Tim Knox, Director of the Royal Collection, and landscape architect Todd Longstaffe-Gowan, relates how in 1741, a bricklayer called Thomas Andrews purchased a seventeenth-century mansion on an 81-year lease under the condition that he demolish it and build three houses on the plot.

Which presumably he did, but only a joined pair of five-bay houses survived – and the two authors bought one of them, called Malplaquet House

Soon after, in 2000, jeweller Romilly and her husband, Charles Saumarez Smith, former chief executive of the Royal Academy of Art, bought the other. This is now romantically secluded behind towering ivy-smothered walls pierced by a full-height wrought-iron gate; but the first time Romilly drove past to look, she could scarcely see it behind a car repair shop stuck on the front.

In the early eighteenth century, a brewing company moved to Mile End, where a young John Charrington joined it in 1766. In 1783 he took over and ran the business with his brother Harry,

who bought Malplaquet House in 1794 and lived there until his death in 1833.

Romilly describes how the wealthy Harry remodelled and enlarged Malplaquet, making two grand rooms each side of the central stairs, and updating the front door and door case. While her own home retains its hearty original glazing bars, Harry remade all his windows with slim bars, then in vogue.

Following Harry's death, the *bon ton* Malplaquet was subdivided and began to skid downhill. Shops stuck on it in 1857 contributed to its slow decline.

Meanwhile Romilly's house, also variously tenanted, met an even crueller fate. In the mid-nineteeth century a coach-builder

PREVIOUS PAGES The dining room is now dado panelled, since the original full-height panelling was lost, but the original scarred and marked overmantel is used to display new pieces of jewellery. Dark shutters and panelling make a perfect foil to a modern Droog chandelier.

OPPOSITE, LEFT It is difficult now to believe that a carriageway was hacked through this house to a workshop, or that the top floor was bombed off. Its sympathetic repair and restoration shows what can be done.

OPPOSITE, RIGHT A weatherboarded extension at the rear houses a lift which allows wheelchair access to all floors, while necessitating only minimal alteration to the structure.

BELOW Old brickwork has been retained, sensitively pieced and patched in with lime-pointed reclaimed bricks where necessary. Sombre-coloured woodwork and a well-chosen lamp are in keeping.

punched an archway through the middle to reach his yard. The front door and door case vanished and the staircase was hacked off. Bodged stairs to the first floor rose from the dining room. The house was divided into left- and right-hand sides and shops were, as with Malplaquet, stuck on the front.

Worse was to come. Following Second World War bomb damage, the entire top floor was taken off. Had the house not been one of a pair it would have been pulled down, but like two people roped in a three-legged race, the houses limped on, with Romilly's house as Malplaquet's stunted sibling: squat, stomach-less, and defaced by slipshod additions.

Before buying it, Romilly and Charles were living in a Georgian house in Limehouse, with Hawksmoor's magnificent St Anne's[2] at the end of the garden, which their two little boys loved. But it was small. 'We kept thinking can we go up, down,

or sideways, but each time we knew it wouldn't work.' Fate stepped in when Charles bumped into their friends, who had just moved to Mile End and told him that the house joined to theirs was for sale.

'Charles went to look, but I said, no way am I going to live in the Mile End Road, it sounds awful.' Romilly smiles. 'Six months later, Todd and Tim invited us to a party and their house was amazing, I couldn't believe the scale of it.'

She rang the Spitalfields Trust, which had bought both derelict houses for a pound from Tower Hamlets council, which planned to knock them down. Part of the deal was that their long back gardens became social housing. After restoring them to a certain point, the Trust would find buyers to finish them.

By the time Romilly and Charles bought their house in 2000, the Trust had removed the run-down shops disgracing the

front and was rebuilding a new top floor, meticulously copying Malplaquet, right down to the brickwork of the chimney stacks.

New walls were soot-rubbed until time and grime could step in. Traditionally skilled craftspeople worked on the restoration, but not an architect – 'just as it would have been done originally', Romilly says approvingly. The long-lost staircase and hall were recreated and an eighteenth-century door case and fanlight found. Panelling was copied and cut in where necessary; floorboards repaired. 'I spent a lot of time on my hands and knees, scrubbing floorboards before they were waxed with beeswax, which we still do three times a year.'

Romilly's brother, joiner Justin Savage, who worked on the house, says that the unusual tapering-twist balusters were turned by the only company left in England able to do it, while the front railings are by Andrew Renwick of Ridgeway Forge,

known for his work at Waddesdon.[3] They frame the huge reclaimed gate beautifully.

The house's ad hoc industrial past had damaged it. The drawing room almost burned down when tyres stored there caught fire. But somehow the burnt panels remained standing. Finding the charred parts beautiful Romilly asked the carpenters to leave them, but one day they replaced a section with fresh timber, which she still masks behind a tall mahogany linen chest.

The floorboards in the chamber above, now the master bedroom, also suffered. She puzzled over their heavy scarred surface, until one day a cab driver bringing her home told her he used to work there when it was a box factory. The box-makers used staple guns, and over time thousands of industrial staples had been misfired into the floor.

OPPOSITE Laying lead on stairs to imitate a stair runner protects the treads and noses, and looks beautiful. This section of the staircase with its fine balusters was carefully copied from its upper parts, which were still intact.

LEFT The sitting room had been used to store tyres for the car repair workshop and had caught fire, superficially burning but not destroying some panelling, which was left *in situ*.

BELOW During a long period of decline and occupancy by various businesses this upper-floor room was used as a wooden-box manufactory. In that time hundreds of the staples used in making the boxes were misfired into the floorboards, leaving remnants and scars.

A contemporary addition is a black weatherboarded lift shaft on the back. It looks just like many eighteenth-century extensions in Spitalfields, but helps Romilly, who uses a wheelchair, while minimally altering the walls of the house. Modest and practical, it is entirely in the spirit of eighteenth-century architecture.

From the outset Romilly did not want to engulf her house in aspic. To that end she hangs modern lighting designed by her and others, calling skeins of lights made from plastic film-canisters her Grinling Gibbons[4] lights. Modern art and furniture sit happily alongside chairs from her grandfather's company, such as two thirties tubs in pelt-print silk velvet rewoven to the original pattern. A small top-floor bedroom has been lined with gold paper, the sheets turned so that the grain catches the light differently, like fabric. The walls shimmer like the ground of a painting by Gustav Klimt.

Romilly's industrious jewellery workshop is tucked inside a former powder room, while her newest pieces of work hang on the dining room overmantel, which bears the nails, gimp and linen on which silk was once fixed. The beautiful wall amplifies the strong impression that the dining room is a painting by Danish artist Wilhelm Hammershøi.

The luminous family home holds so many proofs of a jeweller's hand and eye, placing things and choosing colours. And all in accordance with the way the house was gently re-awoken: 'At first we wondered if too much had been lost, but it was restored very much as it would originally have been done. Things were worked out, using intuition as well as skill.'

1 Tim Knox and Todd Longstaffe Gowan, *Malplaquet House: A Description*, 2008.
2 St Anne's Limehouse by Nicholas Hawksmoor was built in 1727 and consecrated in 1730. It was part of the commission for fifty new churches ratified by Parliament in 1710.
3 Waddesdon Manor in Buckinghamshire was built in the 1870s by Baron Ferdinand de Rothschild.
4 Sculptor Grinling Gibbons (1648–1721) carved in wood. His naturalistic carving, which includes rope-like or festooned arrangements of fruits, flowers, leaves and grain, is highly distinctive.

OPPOSITE, LEFT A detail of the leadwork on the stairs up to the gold bedroom in the attic shows how carefully the flat-headed clouts have been set below the noses, creating an attractive detail in their own right as well as securing the heavy metal.

OPPOSITE, RIGHT Sheets of handmade gold paper originally supplied as samples for the endpapers for a book were laid with their grain in different directions, so that they would catch the light differently, evoking the paintings of Gustav Klimt.

ABOVE Romilly's book-lined office, set in a quiet part of the house and separated from the back stairs by a partition with wavering glass, is a place of artistic inspiration, as well as the comfort provided by a striking yellow-upholstered sofa.

LEFT Purpose-built bookcases in the study are filled with art books but also display a painting and a Staffordshire figure. The strong colours of a modern print of traditional *toile de Jouy* design make the buttoned tub chair stand out.

OPPOSITE, TOP Distinctive tiger-skin silk velvet from Venice is exactly the same as that used on a pair of chairs made by Romilly's grandfather's furniture company, Stenhouse Savage. On the wall, skeins of lights recall the style of Grinling Gibbons.

OPPOSITE, BOTTOM The varied tones of burned, charred and scraped old pine on the original full-height panelling and door, of paint in a warm velvety grey, and of the lustrous silk velvet upholstery are beautiful and harmonious together.

LEFT Within the kitchen hearth the old cast-iron cooking range and fireback make a cool and well-ventilated storage space for fresh eggs and vegetables, and also a tableau worthy of a seventeenth-century Dutch still life.

BELOW Traces left from centuries of old paint layers on this plank door in the basement, combined with the elegance of the original hand-forged hinge, set against limestone slabs, provide examples of both the appeal and the longevity of handmade things.

RIGHT The lines and patination of a torso from a marble figure, set before handmade moudings in the panelling lining to a window embrasure, demonstrate consummate artistry and invite contemplation.

BELOW A partial set of cast-iron cobbler's boot- or shoe-sole lasts in various sizes makes a striking ornament on the hand-hewn dining room hearthstone.

MEN ONLY

WHEN THIS CONVENIENCE
IS CLOSED NEAREST
CONVENIENCES ARE
TURN LEFT INTO MAIN
ROAD AND PROCEED
250 YARDS

A DIFFERENT WAY OF LIVING

The 1790 coaching inn in Shadwell

When film-maker Julian Cole found a large piece of a Roman amphora buried deep in the low, dark beer cellar of his restored 1790 coaching inn in Shadwell, now both his home and a bed-and-breakfast, he felt it was confirmation that 'there had been a purveyor of drink on this spot for two thousand years.'

The glazed terracotta shard is part of his 'museum' in a double-fronted bookcase that holds numerous glass bottles, some whole, more broken, which turned up in an old brick cesspit in the back yard full of glass, crockery and rubbish. Ranging from colourless clear glass to opal-white, pale iridescent green, or deeper blue, many bear the name of a shop or local street, clearly moulded. 'So they could be returned,' Julian explains. In the eighteenth, nineteenth and early twentieth centuries, bottles were generally reused or returned on deposit, a habit that petered out fifty years ago but is now coming back. 'One day we may find out whether there was a nearby manufactory or if they ordered bottles by post.'

One of the fascinations and mysteries of old houses is how things keep turning up and fresh discoveries are made. A large dish in the museum holds innumerable broken clay smoking

PREVIOUS PAGES A former pub sign for the men's 'conveniences' is proudly displayed in the yard. The painter appears to have enjoyed a few pints before tracing out the words.

OPPOSITE, TOP The wall behind the old Victorian bar was moved back, together with its decorative glazing along the top. A cupboard houses a 'museum' of items including old glassware and broken crockery found in the well-made brick cesspit.

OPPOSITE, BOTTOM Scores of bottles, many with the name of the street or the manufacturer moulded in their glass, fill a shelf with their limpid or opalescent greens, whites, aquamarines and dark blues.

BELOW Hundreds of broken clay pipes turned up. Made the same way from the seventeenth into the nineteenth century, their delicate small bowls and long stems broke easily. Such a handsome collection befits an inn.

pipes with long thin necks and small bowls like the puffed-out chests of tiny fledglings. Heaped together they resemble bones. A smaller dish contains what Julian thought were finger bones from some macabre ritual, which he found under the beautiful old floorboards, but they turned out to be from dogs' tails, probably docked for a dog fight on the premises.

In the first-floor living room for guests, huge even with its original parliament-hinged green doors separating off a former small dining room, beneath many layers of wallpaper he found the earliest, a paper of delicate flower sprays on a time-darkened ochre ground. Tenaciously sticking to the old plaster, two hundred years old, it was so pretty that he kept it.

A collector through and through, once Julian had bought the pub in 1997 and made it structurally sound there was a huge space to fill. At first, he retrieved things from skips, including a large wooden settle now covered with Afghan saddle bags. In perfect condition, there it was. Or the kitchen flagstones that

were being lifted up from a nearby alley; or a substantial steel catering unit being wheeled down the road near the London Hospital, [1] ready to be tipped, which he got for £20. 'I had a van in those days and I liked that unit so much that I designed the kitchen round it.' Made from free-standing units the kitchen sits where the former men's toilets were.

When he spots something worth salvaging he is never afraid to ask. Raised for three teenage years on a commune in the countryside where his mother had moved, he discovered that 'there's a different way of living from the nuclear family', and that doing so communally, being cooperative and helpful, is a good way to go through life. He has never forgotten and now, running his b&b in the serene upper floors, in a sense he does so still.

Friends gave him things for his home and new venture: chairs from designer Frick and Frack, which recycles old wood into distinctive items; another pair by architect and designer Nigel Coates, echoing the style. A framed work by film-maker

OPPOSITE The large double sitting room had been papered numerous times, but after the layers were removed one by one the oldest one remained wedded to the 1790s plaster. It was so appealing that it was left.

ABOVE This Victorian settle was found discarded in a skip, in perfect condition. Made more comfortable with Afghan saddle bag cushions, it sits where the women's toilets, a late addition to the inn, once were.

RIGHT The kitchen was designed around a robust steel unit with drawers spotted being wheeled away as rubbish from the Royal London, and acquired for twenty pounds. The rest of the freestanding kitchen has a similarly industrial feel.

BELOW LEFT In the communal living room huge parliament-hinged double doors behind which was once a small dining room are now permanently closed, making a setting for two distinctively French walnut armchairs, upholstered in flame tapestry.

BELOW RIGHT A passageway between the kitchen and the hall of the inn, with the drawing room to the left, houses a collection of carved masks acquired during travels abroad. Beyond, the original mirror advertises the brewer Meux.

Derek Jarman, who once took part in a film of Julian's, and prints by Eduardo Paolozzi, jump out from a kaleidoscopic whirl.

Two Arts and Crafts sideboards, massy as a pair of rhinoceroses in a stand-off, are smothered with finds from trips abroad. A Panasonic radio bears the shiny face of Saddam Hussein; a Cuban puffer fish husk, papery amber against strong sunlight, flares its spikes. 'Four dollars, but *quite* hard to bring back'; tiny *Candomblé*[2] figures from Brazil, and a glorious jumble of masks, carved heads, bits of sculpture, Indonesian shadow puppets. You name it, Julian is quite likely to have it. He had admired similar sideboards in Gilbert and George's house when he spent years making a documentary on their life and work.

He acquired many things at obscure auctions (of which he is a fan), including a stuffed white rabbit dressed in red velvet and ruff.

While living as a poor arthouse film-maker in Hackney he couldn't afford to buy a house there, but realized that pubs were being sold off cheaply elsewhere. He heard of one backing on to Hawksmoor's miraculous church St George in the East (which resembles a sandcastle complete with flag, and delights all who see it).[3] The pub was an enormous 5,000 square feet, but the upper private rooms had been abandoned and the large saloon bar, converted around 1850, was dark and dismal, in use but often empty. There was a men's khazi in the yard.

BELOW, TOP LEFT The dried husk of a poisonous puffer fish, its papery skin glowing like an ambered lantern in the light from the window, only cost four dollars but was rather difficult to transport from Cuba . . .

BELOW, BOTTOM LEFT Among many items brought from other countries and displayed on two immense Arts and Crafts sideboards in the drawing room is a collection of small handmade *Candomblé* figures from Brazil, celebrating a religious dance.

BELOW RIGHT In a home where almost nothing has been bought new from a shop, auctions have played a sometimes unexpected role in providing furnishings. 'I fell in love with Mister Rabbit.' And who would not.

Julian kept checking the estate agent's website and six months later when the pub had been unsold for two years he made a low offer that to his astonishment the owners accepted. For £60,000 he was the proud owner of three tatty floors and a stooping cellar in urgent need of repair, all of which would have to be done on a shoestring, starting with making it habitable. Oddities that turned up included an old train rail ingeniously used as a girder, which he kept, and a women's toilet built inside the bar, right across two south-facing windows. Removing it was the first thing he did, which transformed the feel of the large room. In fact, the beautiful light, which comes from three sides – 'unusual in London' – was the first thing he noticed, and it is the thing he still loves most.

He also noticed original chair-rail wainscot in the upper rooms; and in the former pub saloon, a three-layer ceiling of lath-and-plaster with first Regency and then Victorian match-boarding stuck on top. In the yard, a mysterious little door in the wall led to the site of a former small music hall that was part of the demesne, which may have started life as stabling for the original coaching inn. Sadly, it was long demolished.

Inside, Julian matched old lead paint colours with modern paint, and he repainted the Victorian outside with oil-based paint, to last longer. While the Victorian owners had 'zhuzhed up' the exterior with stucco and glazed tiles, much of the interior was older. Although he dismembered the bar, its rare old pitch pine and mahogany panels found a home in a guest bathroom. He pushed the quarter-glazed panelled screen behind the bar back to enlarge his living room and make a well-proportioned hall for the inn, in which the mirror gilded with the name of the brewer Meux, whose premises were once on Tottenham Court Road where the Dominion Theatre now stands, holds pride of place.

Julian glances at a large nineteenth-century portrait of a handsome fellow in evening dress with hat and gloves, his latest auction find. It didn't cost much, but he liked it. He looks around with a rueful but not repentant smile: 'I never buy new; and I'm better at buying things than I am at getting rid of them.' A lament many owners of old houses will recognize.

The portrait opens an avenue of thought, a door to the past, as do all the other fascinating things he lives among, set in this atmospheric building with its Roman roots. 'Who knows who came here,' he says. 'Oscar Wilde used the opium dens down the road, and Charles Dickens wrote about the spikes along the wall round St George in the East, a few of which I salvaged when they were removed. Either of them could have dropped in for a drink.'

If you look closely, you may glimpse them there still.

1 The Royal London Hospital, Whitechapel, London.
2 A dance in honour of the gods, and an Afro-American religion.
3 Built by Nicholas Hawksmoor between 1715 and 1729.

OPPOSITE While the upper floor of the old coaching inn still looks Georgian, the ground-floor frontage was altered around 1850 with glazed bricks, stucco, and new windows. But the faded brewer's sign still lingers.

BELOW It is difficult to resist the intrigue and mystery of a raddled old door in a raddled old wall. This door leads to the site of a former music hall that was attached to the inn. Bombed in the Second World War, it was subsequently demolished.

OVERLEAF, LEFT The flamboyant mirror brought from behind the bar into the hall proudly advertises wares from the famous Meux's brewery, which was known to have been in business before 1764.

OVERLEAF, RIGHT Under a Victorian tongue-and-groove ceiling in the drawing room hangs a recent auction purchase, a portrait of James Collier Harter of Broughton Hall, painted around 1850. He looks as if he never touched a drop.

WHAT LIES BENEATH

Rediscovering a 1726 house in Spitalfields

PREVIOUS PAGES A horseshoe nailed to the floor by eighteenth-century Huguenot owners to ward off evil spirits.

LEFT The yard of this handsome house endured a spell covered by a workshop. Earlier, in the eighteenth century, the night-soil man came along a now-closed alley to collect sewage.

OPPOSITE A few of the items discovered in the house or garden. Many things had slipped under the floorboards, while a ribbed blue poison bottle with an early syringe had been deliberately concealed behind a false panel, and a child's set of porcelain jacks was found under a stone step. Larger objects included a silver thimble, a bottle with its original label exquisitely handwritten with a steel nib, and an almost complete clay pipe, beautifully designed with an integral stand.

A colt-sized horseshoe set into a floorboard as a Huguenot way to discourage evil spirits from crossing a threshold; a tiny hand-stitched leather shoe tucked in a hearth to do the same; Victorian ceramic jacks beneath the stoop; a ribbed blue poison bottle and early steel hypodermic behind a panel; and gold embroidery thread, jet buttons and nylon thread tumbling from an old rat's nest in a cascade worthy of a modern artist. Just a few of the small items discovered in John and Juliano's house during John's ten-year conservation and restoration after buying the house in the mid-1990s. John is a journalist and broadcaster, Juliano a translator, and as in an archaeological version of *La Ronde*, they recognize that they too have lost things below floorboards or in the yard – a coin or a cufflink – for another inhabitant to discover a century from now.

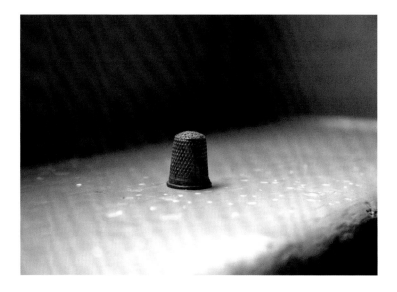

When John bought the five-storey 1720s terrace house, the surrounding area was very different. In 1991, the last few market traders had left Spitalfields' famous fruit and vegetable market, there since 1638, yet the nearby Market Café still kept market hours. 'It opened at midnight, with steaming vats of stew and bubble-and-squeak for traders who never came,' John recalls. Street-walkers, down-and-outs and night owls queued for egg rolls and hot drinks. 'A man in a long Dickensian coat used to walk about and open his coat as if he was flashing – but he wasn't: watches for sale were pinned to the linings.'

John had been renting in Notting Hill, where it was too expensive to buy even a small flat. He knew the village-like group of beautiful but derelict old houses in East London, many boarded up. Anyone with an ounce of romance in their soul who remembers that time will instantly picture those cobbled and flagged streets, peppered with early eighteenth-century houses whose colour appeared to have seeped from them and which seemed to be slumbering, dreaming wistfully of rescue.

Using the Land Registry, John tracked down absentee owners and sent them letters of interest. One agreed to sell – a bank, from which he bought his future home 'for a pittance'. His own bank considered his purchase folly.

One of a pair, the large ten-room terrace house consisted of basement, three floors and an attic, with two rooms per floor, a common pattern. It began life as a well-to-do silk-weaver's or silk merchant's house. In the early nineteenth century a wooden shop front had been put across both houses, but only John's retained it. The house had been tenanted, then the tenants bought it. Later, it was used in the rag trade, as were many houses in the area. A warehouse or workshop went up in the yard. At one point a tailor worked on the second floor, and in the thirties, an old lady lived in what is now the rear attic bathroom, a tiny but charming room beneath steep eaves. She must have cooked supper on the grate, and flung the contents of her chamber pot from the casement windows.

There was no electricity, no water and no gas, although once there would have been gas lighting, John says. When he demolished the workshop, black-and-yellow spiders, perhaps from a nearby banana importer, scurried off, and pig bones emerged that looked human enough to catch the eye of a police officer who dropped in out of interest on her beat. As did an overgrown lane behind the houses, used by the night-soil man to cart away sewage.[2]

'As a child I loved old houses. When I was about seven, I used to creep into a grand old Victorian mansion with horsehair sofas and a mangle and a cooking range. I begged my parents to buy it and restore it. They refused, but I swore I'd do it one day.'

When John at last went inside his Spitalfields house, the staircase was swinging away from the wall. In the ground-floor rooms metal panels were screwed on the internal walls, he believes as a fire prevention measure. To fit them flush the chair-rails had been hacked off, along with all internal shutters and rim-locks. A sweatshop had run electricity on a cable twisted round the balusters, leaving scorch marks.

While gingerly exploring he stumbled across a hatch to the basement – a surprise, for he didn't know there was one. By flashlight he edged down into a space so deep with rubbish he couldn't stand up. He found himself in the original kitchen, complete with its large hearth for cooking. The internal staircase to it had collapsed.

For a few years he lived in the attic, cooking on the fire and doing the clearing and stripping himself, until he met local

OPPOSITE This room, now a romantic bathroom under the eaves, was once lived in by an elderly lady who cooked in the tiny grate and threw slops out of the window. New designs, including a Tom Dixon Jack Light, make a chic foil for the old.

RIGHT At different periods in its almost 300-year existence the house has undergone many stylistic modifications. This curved hall wall with neatly fitted head-and-butt dado panelling is probably Victorian.

BELOW The original basement kitchen had been filled with rubbish. The lightwell was blocked up and the internal staircase had collapsed. Once dug out the kitchen was furnished using old ledge-and-brace cupboards that had graced a Norfolk toolshed, and a table that had been sent to salvage by Harrods Furniture Depository. The lovely 1940s aluminium kettle was bought at Spitalfields Antiques Market.

craftspeople accustomed to old houses. 'All talented eccentrics', he says fondly. The house was freezing. His refuge was a dwarf post bed made by the local joiner.

Every original ceiling had a false one nailed over its bumpy lath and horsehair. During the Second World War, the attic rooms had had what were intended to be bomb-proof ceilings added. As he removed them they collapsed one by one, showering him with bits and pieces trapped between the joists: 'The history of the house tumbled through, from children's toys to nineteenth-century coins and wedding rings.'

As he peeled the layers back he realized that the rooms were taller than he had first thought. And as the metal panels and then the plastic wood covering the first-floor walls came off, he saw panelling, some dado height and some full height, along with some

good carved wooden cornices in the first-floor drawing rooms, plus original doors, and grates made by Carron[3] in Scotland, boarded up inside intact fireplaces 'full of mussel shells and small oyster shells, the fast food of the eighteenth-century poor'.

OPPOSITE The wide original stairs, now lovingly polished and the risers sensibly painted mahogany against scuffs, make a good display place for curiosities that include a decorator's wood-grain roller and a pair of seventeenth-century Ottoman leather men's shoes.

BELOW LEFT An eighteenth-century rush-bottomed ladderback chair sits well against the chair-rail of the first-floor landing panelling. Mounting toggle light switches in Perspex minimizes their visual effect.

BELOW RIGHT Small corner sinks are fairly common on the upper floors of these houses, which were often in multiple occupancy in the nineteenth and twentieth centuries.

LEFT This magnificent late-nineteenth-century gilded mirror was a gift from the owner of an Italian palazzo. Placed between the windows, it dazzlingly reflects a collection of Scandinavian glass candlesticks. The Eames sofa was found on the street.

OPPOSITE In the music room the crisp lines of a 1960s harpsichord and the splendour of a nineteenth-century Indian worked silver chair continue the harmonious and successful mixture of old and new furnishings.

1 *La Ronde*: A 1950s French film based on an 1897 play by Arthur Schnitzler. A chain of stories link, repeat and return in a merry-go-round parable about human life.
2 In the eighteenth century and until the widespread installation of flushing lavatories in the nineteenth and even twentieth centuries, so-called night soil men collected night soil – faeces – sometimes by dedicated back alleys or paths. Joseph Bramah patented a flushing water closet in 1778, but it was a long time before they were installed in any but wealthy houses.
3 Carron was set up in 1759 in Falkirk, Stirlingshire and famously made cannons. In the nineteenth century it became one of the largest ironworks in Europe, celebrated for decorative ironwork ranging from grates to bath tubs.

When he cleaned the windows, which were as opaque as cardboard, he found a house much brighter than the dingy brown one he began with.

The walls had been wallpapered more often than painted. Among many examples that John documented and stored were some fragments whose pattern an expert dated to the 1690s: a costly commodity, probably hung by the first owners. 'It seemed that it was a much finer house than I had envisaged,' he says.

But there were difficult decisions to make, such as whether to keep the nineteenth-century shop front. Since John's house was one of a pair with a shared door case, and the neighbouring frontage had been reverted to a domestic eighteenth-century exterior, for a sense of unity and visual harmony he did the same.

Such choices, which involve soul-searching, had to be made repeatedly. John kept the hall's nineteenth-century tongue-and-groove half-panelling, while in the drawing room, since there

were excellent remnants of cornice and panelling, he used them as patterns to restore the whole room.

Today, the house is full of mid-twentieth-century modern furniture. 'We are inveterate eBayers and auction-trawlers,' he says, smiling at Juliano. 'When I moved in I had very little money. At that time nobody wanted the house, but I could afford it and I liked it. Now, I could probably sell it and replace it with eighteenth-century furniture, with money left over.'

John thought long and hard about the best way to repair his home. 'There is an ongoing debate between conservation and restoration, and you have to decide what you like, because logically there have been three centuries since this house was built, and you can't restore them all. You must muddle through. I wanted the house to look as if it had aged gently, like a glamorous, elegant old actress – not as if it had had a brutal facelift.'

FIT FOR A QUEEN

An important 1726 silk-weaver's house in Spitalfields

'There was a moment when there were no floors at all,' says Ben Adler, who since the death of his wife, Pat Llewellyn, lives with his dog Edith, a rambunctious Australian Shepherd, in the house he and Pat painstakingly restored together in Spitalfields. As Ben puts it, the house that they bought thinking it only needed a coat of paint 'suddenly went to a skeleton'. The wine cellar had been filled with concrete, which took one man a month to remove with a pneumatic drill, and the house needed considerable structural work. 'To put in steels, the builders took up all the boards; there was no roof, we could see the sky.

'That was when we thought, maybe we shouldn't have done it,' Ben muses.

Film producers Ben and Pat learned hands-on the surprises that a very old building can spring, but the finished beauty of their large red-brick, four-bay, five-storey house justifies the years they lavished on bringing it back to life, and their attention to the smallest detail.

With its imposing central portico and door case the house was built in 1726, and was first lived in by its builder, William Tayler. Tayler, a carpenter, is also thought to have built the impressive oak staircase with pretty carved motifs, lit up and down by a south-facing two-storey window on the first landing. From it, sunlight shafts across the Portland stone hall floor that Pat and Ben installed to a traditional cabochon pattern, in which octagonal flags are diapered with black squares. According to Ben, the Victoria and Albert Museum once tried to buy the rare staircase, but luckily for the house didn't succeed. The monumental structure was in such good condition that apart from small repairs only one small section had to be re-carved; it was done so well, by a Polish carpenter, that no one notices.

Originally this was one of the middle-sized houses in the area. Silk merchants who lived resplendent in nearby Spital Square owned the grandest, but they are now lost, and this house became one of the biggest by default. In its long life it has had many owners, some documented. The majority worked in the silk industry, during which time doors cut through the brickwork connected it to the neighbouring property to make vast weaving workshops. Silk was woven; some believe that the silk-satin known to have been woven in Spitalfields for Queen Victoria's wedding dress was loomed here. While Ben has not seen any document to confirm it, it is easy to imagine. In 1840, the house became a school, and later a home for 'working boys'.

'It seemed ridiculous to me that you could actually buy a house like this, which felt more like a stately home,' Ben says, recalling the wintry day in 2012 that he first saw it. He and Pat lived in

PREVIOUS PAGES Two pilasters flanking the high, grand entrance hall have unusual, mainly Ionic capitals that also feature coy bunches of grapes and a stylized acanthus leaf motif.

RIGHT Similarly complicated motifs grace the carved wooden three-quarter pillars beneath the lead-hooded recessed portico on the door case of this fine four-bay house, which has been very carefully conserved and restored throughout.

BELOW Beautifully pleached mature pear trees make a dramatic focal point for the large courtyard garden that has been created around an ancient mulberry tree.

LEFT A dramatic view from the top of the house down through the oblong stairwell to the opulent flourish of the curved curtail. This important staircase was probably made by the house's builder and first owner, William Tayler.

BELOW LEFT Turned and twisted oak balusters, three to each tread, supporting a fine broad mahogany handrail, are further embellished with carvings of scrolling stylized leaves and flowers on the oak tread-brackets.

OPPOSITE, LEFT AND RIGHT On the top landing a mural painted by Argentinian artist Ricardo Cinalli features a bold view of a naked man from below. The more modest section here shows an equally naked spaniel on a marbled ground. Edith, the Australian Shepherd, sits on an *almost* marbled ground made of Portland stone hall tiles diapered with slate in a classical pattern.

Camden, in a house they found soulless despite fifteen dogged years trying to improve it. Moreover, 'the area was full of children and buggies, which felt strange, as we were childless.' A friend told them about a house for sale in Spitalfields, but since Ben's only previous experience of the area was of a small, low-ceilinged house where he couldn't stand upright in the kitchen (he is six-foot-seven), he wasn't in a hurry to look. However, what they eventually saw convinced him. Every room was enormous and every ceiling, even in the basement, which held a gym and sauna, and a wall curiously dividing a hearth in two, was high enough to stand up under. And although the house looked tired, it still had grace.

They rented nearby and a survey was done. Since the house had stood for almost three hundred years and they were assured that it might stand for three hundred more, the couple felt no need to rush with their grand and exciting new project.

In November 2013, Pat was diagnosed with cancer. They decided to get on with the restoration.

A second survey revealed that the house was supported by great beams running front to back on every floor. A fire in the 1960s had damaged a crucial one that helped support the first floor, and so the building above it. But the surveyor took stock and suggested propping followed by substantial steelwork.

Ben laughs, although it may not have seemed funny at the time. 'There's an amazing amount of steel now, so even if a bomb dropped on it, it wouldn't fall down. It's helpful for parties, because I never worry about the floor collapsing.'

The couple spent a long time finding an architect who would restore the house the way they wanted it done, using lath and plaster and traditional techniques. For as Ben points out, 'a wonky floor won't work with a straight ceiling.' Over time the house has slipped and slid to one side then the other, and gone up and down a bit, like a galleon on a gentle swell; and door architraves and doors and panels have been recut and adjusted to suit different levels. Taken all together this adds wonderful charm – but takes a great deal of skill to sort out.

They chose Julian Harrap, who had restored Sir John Soane's Museum[1] and many buildings of similar ilk. His team of craftspeople, from carpenters to masons to plasterers, were accustomed to wonky houses and familiar with using hairy lime plaster and laying lath, a painstaking process.

It took a year to get every detail passed by the planners, which must be done with all but superficial changes to a listed house, even Grade II. Grade II is the most ordinary category, and a broad church, which consequently contains the vast majority of listed houses.

At last, they began the slow, patient work, which took three years.

Historic England[2] took an interest in the repair of this very fine house, for while there are a great many Grade II houses in this part of East London in particular, each one is infinitely valuable, which must always be borne in mind.

OPPOSITE The attic bedroom's small windows were replaced by a run of generous metal weavers' windows, which have a direct view to the building known as the Gherkin. In a house where every floor and every lath-and-plaster ceiling is wonky, this ceiling is spectacularly so.

RIGHT The delightful Delft tiles behind this sink with French lop-eared taps came from a suitcase of eighty mixed tiles from Hooton Pagnell, bought at a Bonhams house-contents auction. They have been used here and there throughout the house.

BELOW LEFT The old iron pillar and ancient original beam, curved with the ceiling, are now part of an unobtrusive and highly engineered support system for the house to counter structural damage that was probably caused during the 1960s.

BELOW RIGHT One of the first pieces of art Ben ever bought was a concrete triptych by sculptor Mick Thacker. It is installed over the enormous bath (which took several men to lug up to the top).

LEFT A very fine collection of hand-whittled Welsh cawl spoons. These large-bowled spoons (sometimes mistaken for love spoons) were traditionally used to eat a hearty Welsh broth called cawl. Many people still delight in using them.

RIGHT The kitchen had been subdivided long before. Ben and Pat reopened it, flagged it with gigantic slabs from a station in Yorkshire, and moved in a massive bespoke kitchen island and four ovens. Made for cooking and entertaining, this is an extremely practical room.

Even the original front-door fanlight caused discussions. When the couple bought their house the fanlight was conspicuous by its absence, and the then timber-floored hall commensurately gloomy. Fortunately, they found it stored downstairs, though with broken glass. Ben reckons that it had probably been in and out of the door several times as fashions changed; but its presence on site helped their argument for its reinstatement.

The couple moved in in November 2016. 'Pat lived in terror of waking up in a museum rather than a comfortable home, so it was all about making a twenty-first-century home in a Georgian house.' Ben smiles; and it is impossible not to smile at the memory of his very talented and humorous wife, who produced unforgettable television from Jamie Oliver to *Two Fat Ladies*, and who died in October 2017.

Whether it was restoring the glass, for which they chose a handmade Victorian style for its particularly appealing wobble;

or hauling huge Yorkshire flags (which came from an old railway station) down to the basement; whether it was putting in four ovens and a huge wooden island, because the couple loved entertaining and knew how to do it well; whether it was remaking steel weavers' windows for the loft bedrooms, or sourcing a suitcaseful of rare seventeenth- and eighteenth-century Delft tiles for splashbacks and elsewhere, this house has been transformed by love and is a testament to what love can achieve.

At an attic window looking towards the City, Ben says, 'this is my favourite view: standing in a soon-to-be-300-year-old house gazing at the Gherkin. It is a Bladerunner-like scene.'

1 In Lincoln's Inn Fields, London, the former home, now house-museum, of architect and collector Sir John Soane (1753-1837) who famously built the Bank of England and Dulwich Picture Gallery.
2 Historic England, formerly English Heritage, is the public body that looks after England's historic environment.

LEFT Gilt-embellished mercury glass reflects Pat Llewellyn's numerous BAFTAs and other awards, won during a career of producing groundbreaking food and cookery programmes. The eighteenth-century black Kilkenny marble fire surround sets them off.

BELOW LEFT Great care was taken over the details of all fittings, from taps to rim-locks. This particularly attractive engraved brass rim-lock gleams invitingly on the door to the first-floor drawing room.

RIGHT The large drawing room was repartitioned, with full-height doors. Modern and eighteenth-century paintings mixed with comfortable furniture, such as this velvet-upholstered sofa, make a glamorous entertaining space.

A DUTCH STILL LIFE

A picturesque 1794 house in South London

Few expressions are as instantly evocative as these three words: Dutch still life. The darkness, the stillness, the flowers or books or objects, vividly and realistically painted in the seventeenth-century, the whole brought alive by a gilded frame. And so it is in art historian Frank Hollmeyer's five-storey Georgian house in a pretty square in South London, which he and his boyfriend, Robert Weems, stumbled across when they took the wrong turn on an evening stroll. The entire house is a still life that Frank dedicates his free time to perfecting. Since his period is seventeenth-century Dutch, he knows how to position a Delft tulip jar and a few books on a small table in an irresistible way. 'I love recreating a seventeenth-century interior, like those of Pieter de Hooch:[1] very domestic, very inward-looking, very concentrated,' he says.

Yet his house is also easy to live in; for comfort, cooking, and entertaining. That is imperative to Frank, who has made it warm and inviting throughout. Sofas are covered in thick sweet-smelling linen with plump cushions; floors do not creak, and all the radiators work. There is even a modern bathroom, although traditional brass taps add elegance and a soft golden glow.

'We were looking for something bigger. I had a small Regency house in Islington and wanted to stay in that area. Definitely not South London as we didn't know it at all.' But on that fateful stroll they were just walking past an attractive house in a square, with neat railings and an original fanlight, when the door opened. A young man came out, tied a 'For Sale' sign to the railings, and went in again.

PREVIOUS PAGES A Clerkenwell harpsichord-maker showed the proper way to restore and gild old frames. One of these was bought in Vienna.

LEFT A long, painstaking reconstruction involved building new shutters and shutter boxes, and copying fire surrounds and cornices from an *in situ* section, 'to get the bones of the house right', as here in the elegantly comfortable ground-floor drawing room.

RIGHT These two Robert Adam plaster-on-wood pilaster capitals had been stored since the 1920s in a barn, after being removed from a house to make room for an art deco ballroom. Decades later the capitals, which survived bombing during the war, were sold to salvage.

The following day Frank rang up to enquire, and learned that it was a private sale. A couple had bought the house from the council twenty-eight years earlier and raised their family in it. Now the children were grown up and one, a son, wanted to be an estate agent, so his father had suggested that he try selling it.

In this way, and in a mere three weeks – which is perhaps how quickly houses were bought and sold in past centuries – Frank and Robert decamped to South London after all.

Half German and half Dutch, Frank has lived and studied in many countries, but when he was six he lived in Limburg in South Holland, where many streets were named after Dutch painters. 'I was always wondering who those people were.' At eighteen, he lived in Amsterdam: 'It had been the trading centre of the world and was all laid out and planned, not higgledy-piggledy like London. I thought the grandeur of the architecture

and layout was magnificent. And, of course, William and Mary[2] brought that style here, and what is Georgian architecture except a derivative of seventeenth-century architecture?'

The rigour of that style impressed him and was one of the attractions of his own house. For while the proportions are beautiful and the spaces naturally lit by large windows, it has tremendous natural elegance – yet the basic brick-and-timber design is simple, pragmatic, almost austere.

However, when Frank bought it in 2011, its beauty was concealed under a rather large bushel of late-twentieth-century additions: carpets, pine fire surrounds, and woodchip wallpaper. 'This area used to be a slum,' he explains. 'If you look it up on Booth's Poverty Map[3] from the nineteenth century, it is all black. The area was so poor that twenty or thirty people lived in one house. In the 1930s the council compulsorily purchased many

of these houses and this was one of a pair they knocked together into lateral flats. All the shutters and shutter boxes were ripped out, almost all the cornices, dados, the fireplaces. Every other front door went, so I was lucky that mine escaped. False ceilings went in over the lath-and-plaster ones. When we restored the house, we found layers of fifties kitchen wallpaper in the plaster-cast room behind the sitting room.'

He would also find, when he prepared to decorate his bedroom at the top of the house in spectacular neoclassical[4] fashion, an uncomfortably low ceiling. The builders took it down and found that the true ceiling was six inches higher, supported by a massive beam running front to back. This joyous thing had been completely invisible. Frank found out that it was a ship's timber from Chatham Royal Docks. 'Good timber was valuable,' he says, 'so when ships were

decommissioned, these great lengths were sold for house-building.' Indeed, at close intervals along its sides are slim slots perhaps cut to take decking.

It was very important to Frank to make the house lovely in every part. He decided to start at the bottom and work his way up, but at one point he ran out of money so had to wait a year before starting again. In the first phase he took out all the

OPPOSITE A collection of plaster casts displayed on a muted ground. They come from France, Antwerp and Vienna; some from nineteenth-century engineering or art schools where they were used as exemplars, others by modern master Peter Hone.

BELOW In the neoclassical bedroom, influenced by French styles from 1810 to 1830, the arresting handblocked grisaille panel of Psyche taking a bath was printed with thirteen different greys, using wooden blocks made in the nineteenth century.

modern additions, then cleaned, repaired, and washed the floors translucent grey, which unifies them; reinstated the dado rail, and found one piece of original cornice, which his builders were able to build a mould from and then recast. This was a piece of great good fortune. He also rebuilt all the missing shutter boxes and shutters, a lengthy process, and slightly raised the opening between sitting room and plaster-cast room, which instantly lightens both spaces.

By chance he had recently met Tim Whittaker, whose house features on pages 126–139. 'Tim is so passionate about old houses, and knows so much, it is infectious,' Frank says. Tim visited the house and then sketched fire surrounds and moulding details for the builders to work from.

On the first floor in the back room, Frank wanted a room that looked about 1792, so here Tim drew a massy timber cornice, and panelling to go over the fireplace. Once the room was finished, Frank painted it a purplish shade. A pale, painted Gustavian[5] desk and chairs from his former house look well against it.

Once the first fix was done the kitchen went in. Where many Georgian house owners use flagstones, Frank chose small square handmade French terracotta tiles called *tomettes*. Their soft, almost chalky orange-pink-lemon tones are also very Dutch. Then he built a simple, plain kitchen, but there is no mistaking the efficiency of the big modern range cooker, or the gleaming copper pans, for he is a serious cook.

Finally, he laid out the garden in formal seventeenth-century Dutch style with several compartments; the idea of garden rooms is a very old one. In the first, closest to the house, and appearing enamel-like from the upper windows, formal brick walkways are set around a geometric parterre laid to tulips. A second garden

OPPOSITE Collected over the years, these sculptural Georgian lead-crystal neck-ring decanters grouped on an eighteenth-century mahogany wine table refract light wonderfully, making one of the many informal still lifes around the house.

RIGHT Dutch still lifes are a source of inspiration, especially the paintings of Pieter de Hooch. But here, a flopping hyacinth and hairy twine knotted around a Parisian edition of William Thackeray's 1852 novel *Henry Esmond* evoke a more playful mood.

BELOW Whether it is a carriage lamp on the wall, or pretty *tomettes* on the floor, nothing is unconsidered here; yet with its steel range arrayed with copper pans and the island beneath modern caged pendants, the charming kitchen is designed for utility.

is separated from the first by pleached crab apples and a small hedge of young copper beech. He is working on a third and final space to dine in, divided by a row of sapling hornbeams standing staunchly upright like little whips.

How things sit together, how they look and feel, all matter when creating something as particular as this house. The result of Frank's work is hugely enjoyable, and not just for the eyes – although that would recompense most of us.

'I do this because it gives me intense pleasure to use beautiful things,' he says. 'When a silver knife touches Meissen porcelain it makes a very special sound. That is the sensory experience of genuine things. Or cooking with copper. The pans are a nightmare to clean, but they look beautiful, and the way they spread the heat is unique. Everything here has already been recycled by other owners, probably many times, It is a rewarding, environmentally friendly way to live, and makes a very small carbon footprint.'

Who could argue with that?

1 Pieter de Hooch (1629–1684) was a Dutch painter of highly detailed mainly domestic interiors.
2 Co-Regents of England, Ireland and Scotland, William III and Mary II reigned 1689–1702. William was Dutch, Mary, his first cousin, English.
3 Map Descriptive of London Poverty, 1898–1899, by Charles Booth, in which areas were coloured or shaded according to relative wealth. The black areas were the ones Booth identified as the poorest.
4 Neoclassical: A stylistic movement drawing on classical designs, which began around 1750.
5 A distinctive Swedish style during the reigns of Kings Gustav III and IV of Sweden, from 1771–1809.

OPPOSITE, TOP LEFT, TOP RIGHT & BELOW An albino turtle shell — an example of those used in the nineteenth century as firebacks; a Gustavian desk from a Rothschild château; all in a sophisticated deep lavender study. Gustavian chairs match the desk, and two Chinese ginger jars stand in front of the fireplace, whose surround was designed to give an air of the late Georgian period.

BELOW The knot garden of clipped geometric box firmly enclosing jubilant swathes of colourful tulips recreates a seventeenth- or eighteenth-century Dutch townhouse garden — much more formal than its English equivalent, where romanticism held sway.

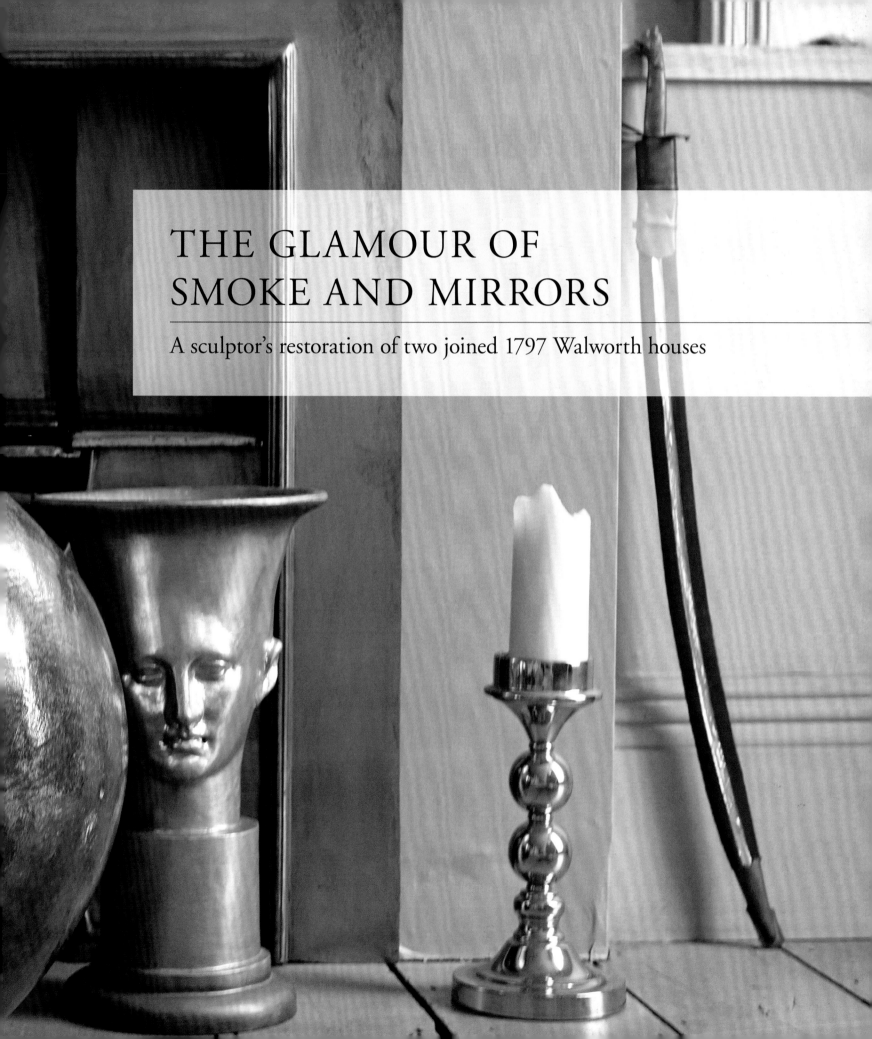

THE GLAMOUR OF
SMOKE AND MIRRORS

A sculptor's restoration of two joined 1797 Walworth houses

PREVIOUS PAGES One of Oriel's instantly recognizable 'theatrical baroque' sculptures, a ceramic vase made for a party, sits flanked by a large lustred ceramic ball made for an abandoned chandelier project, before a repro-Regency steel fire surround bought in the Old Kent Road.

LEFT The formerly unpromising yard was transformed into a baroque fantasy, roped in wisteria and populated by a pair of putti and one of two magnificent ceramic tulip vases, which Oriel made in sections, as each whole was too heavy for one person to move.

BELOW In the workshop, a former garage full of cleaning supplies, Oriel models and casts; these days using fibreglass rather than breakable china. Storage boxes are piled high with plaster moulds for enticingly named mermen/maids, and a lion man.

OPPOSITE The sitting room is dominated by two gold swans cast as table ornaments; sofas in Venetian-patterned gold velvet bought online; and a Regency portrait of Ginger Boyd by Sir Martin Archer Shee, dented when it fell off a car on the way back from auction.

Few people have the talent or the energy of sculptor Oriel Harwood, whose instantly recognizable chandeliers, torchons, épergnes, tables and ceramics first made her international reputation in the early 1990s. She calls her flamboyant and generally large style 'theatrical baroque'.

Oriel is both modest and humorously dismissive about her work, despite the scale and finish of the many pieces that she makes in a studio within her high-walled yard. A former shed, the studio's exterior now resembles a French pavilion with mirrors and trellis, while the inside is artistically organized mayhem. Here she makes moulds, casts fibreglass, and prepares ceramics to fire. Outside in the yard stand a pair of gigantic and very striking mauve-purple and white tulip vases from a series done years ago. One got broken when a magazine borrowed the pair for a shoot and returned them in cardboard boxes with no padding: 'I thought someone had stamped on it.' Unfazed, Oriel glued it back together. Each four-foot vase comes apart, as the whole is too heavy for one person to lift.

Since then she prefers to work in fibreglass – as she did with a pair of gold swans in the sitting room. She spotted one in a shop, a glass table top stuck on its head. She made a mould from it, cast its twin in reverse, and painted them both gold. Now the eye-catching pair guard the fireplace. Oriel shrugs, as if this is the sort of thing we all do.

Perhaps it is no surprise that in her 1797 home in Walworth, shared with her husband, Keith Taylor, a retired book editor, and their Shihtzu, Morticia, she applied the same vigorous creative flair. Twenty-two years of restoration and decoration have transformed a pair of languishing five-storey houses into a work of art. All on a small budget, much of the work done by Oriel herself.

The scale and breadth of what she has done are remarkable, particularly given the condition the houses were in.

Apart from chandeliers and other sculptural pieces throughout the now double, symmetrical house, Oriel made *scagliola* floors, tables and fire surrounds; designed mirrors, painted walls; designed her gilded post-bed and dressing room; and made curtains and bed hangings from colourful fabric bought at Southall market. The result is a glittering environment, which has a striking visual sympathy with its rather Regency character, but in an original, inspiring and unpompous way.

In 1995, Oriel and her first husband lived in a small house two minutes down the road. For six years they'd noticed the decrepit houses forming the end of a Regency terrace. Boarded up, with a big sign of cast iron and Perspex that advertised a printing works and another that read 'Trespassers Will Be Prosecuted', they were hard to miss.

Eventually, Oriel made an offer. Two months later, for little more than the price of their single house, she and her husband owned the derelict conjoined pair.

'The joined house had stopped being residential in 1880,' Oriel explains. 'After that it was a school, then a posh pram factory, then a cleaning contractor.

'It was ghastly,' she adds with expletive-enhanced gusto. 'The front was splattered with Tyrolean render that looked like

apricot oatmeal. One front door had been plasterboarded over and rendered. When we broke through, it was like going into Tutankhamun's tomb.

'Inside there was textured wallpaper, vinyl flooring, and polystyrene ceiling tiles. It was absolutely awful. Just before it was listed in 1972, everything had been ripped out: fireplaces, cornices – all gone. My future studio was piled up with chemicals used by the cleaning contractor.'

Since the house had long been a single building, one staircase was gone, too, and all the balusters had been taken off the remaining one. To lay vinyl floors, the old boards had been levelled with a caustic compound that ate into them. They all needed replacing.

OPPOSITE The magnificent bed was designed, embellished, and painted gold, then hung with fabrics in the glorious colours of Indian miniatures: a palette of Indian or Chinese yellow, searing pink and emerald. The curtain fabric cost £10 from Southall.

BELOW LEFT The golden elephant was bought at discount, and then a friend cut it in half with a chainsaw to flank the bed. Exotic prints are set in frames copied from a Moroccan one given by designer and painter Lawrence Mynott.

BELOW RIGHT Between bedroom and bathroom there runs a voluptuous mirrored dressing room entirely gilded with Dutch gold leaf, an alloy that imitates true gold. Opulent brocaded or embellished garments further enrich the jewel-like room.

And concrete tiles on the roof were weighing down the entire structure: 'We knew they would have to be changed quite quickly.'

On the plus side, the old sash windows were there, including full-length ones on the first floor, with boarded-over shutter boxes and shutters. The building was fundamentally sound – an indication of the robust nature of Georgian houses. And because the roof did not let in water, there was no woodworm. Oriel also discovered some reeded Regency architrave, which she had remade throughout.

Breaking through the horrible render to find the front door 'was a piece of joy, for to recreate it with fanlight and pilasters would cost telephone numbers. But the buggers had taken the knocker off.' Thoughtfully, she adds: 'They did very weird things.'

There was no heating and little money, so at first the couple survived in the attic, keeping warm with fan heaters. After stripping the basement back to brick and laying flagstones, they moved downstairs. Then they split up. 'There I was in 1998, with an enormous Georgian wreck that I desperately wanted to keep.'

And Oriel did keep it. 'But the truth about an old house,' she says, 'is that you don't uncover lots of wonderful details and bits of cornice, you uncover polystyrene tiles, usually painted orange. The colour schemes here were from the sixties and the seventies. There was a staff room in the basement straight out of the seventies, with brown lozenge wallpaper and a purple ceiling.'

All that would have daunted many people, but her upbringing was tailormade for just such a job. 'My parents were proto-neo-Georgians. Their first house was a Victorian farmhouse that they Georgianified because they couldn't afford real Georgian. Then in the early sixties they bought a house in Suffolk that had a Repton[1]-designed garden and a folly. My father enjoyed driving down promising-looking driveways, One day he spotted a house from 1560 with a 1480 hall house attached to it. They bought it. I remember him standing in the kitchen, where all the brickwork had fallen out of the timber framing. He wasn't bothered at all. He used shipwrights to restore the hall, because they understood timber. So I knew old houses and was relatively fearless about what one can and cannot do.'

Because her house had been almost completely gutted, Oriel felt that she could replace some missing surface details with some of her own design, as long as they were done in the spirit of the house. Yet, while she has indeed made some notable and removable additions, such as a powerful black-and-gold scagliola fire surround that perfectly imitates a fancy marble, in the end she did much less than she anticipated. 'One must have respect for the fabric of the house and repair what remains,' she says, 'and *then* decide what to do.'

Therefore, her additions, done with great skill and flair, are mainly decorative.

She made great use of paint, helped by relatives, friends and students, using big cans of oil paint mixed locally. The huge double drawing room is a tour de force of Regency-cum-1920s glamour, with mirrored alcoves she designed; steel fireplaces, floorboards whitewashed to resemble lime-wax, and luminous pale blue-grey and stone-colour walls, doors, and skirting boards, to which the reeded architrave provides an ideal foil and framing device. The furnishings are online finds that she re-covered and touched up with gold paint. It's a perfect setting for her glorious silvered chandeliers and silver-lustre Grotesque vases set rhythmically on rough plaster plinths. Imitation silver-fox rugs add a flamboyant final touch.

Flamboyance and style is what this house is about. It has been carefully and lovingly done, with a judicious and sensitive awareness of what can and what should not be attempted.

She recalls how, in 1998, a structural engineer looked the house over and said: 'Once in every hundred years a house needs a decent owner and, fortunately for this house, Oriel, that's you.'

'And I thought, oh, *shit*.'

1 Humphry Repton, 1752–1818, a Suffolk-born English landscape designer.

LEFT The palatial entertaining space has mirrored alcoves, silvered candelabra and Grotesque vases all designed by Oriel, who also washed the floors a silvery tone and painted the chairs to imitate gilt. Fake silver-fox rugs complete the fairytale.

ABOVE Neatly applied gold and silver paint works illusionistic, elegant wonders on the curvaceous legs of this pale moiré-taffeta-upholstered French chair with pretty tufted trimmings, turning it into a fantasy chariot fit for a prince or princess.

LEFT A well-judged balance of colour and texture means that even small details contribute a great deal. The reeded oval knob complements the reeded architrave, while wallpaper in imitation crocodile leather conjures a whiff of exotic smoking room.

BELOW Deep chocolate-brown oil paint on the floor and woodwork gives the large library a brooding air. Reeded display vitrines are filled with sourcebooks as well as skulls, eggs, shells, and many other sculptural fragments, creating a true cabinet of curiosities.

OPPOSITE In the tapestry room a substantial velvet-upholstered Regency mahogany chair sports its trailing gimp and tatters of velvet in front of a lovely copy of an eighteenth-century tapestry from Brussels of a wild boar hunt (a gift).

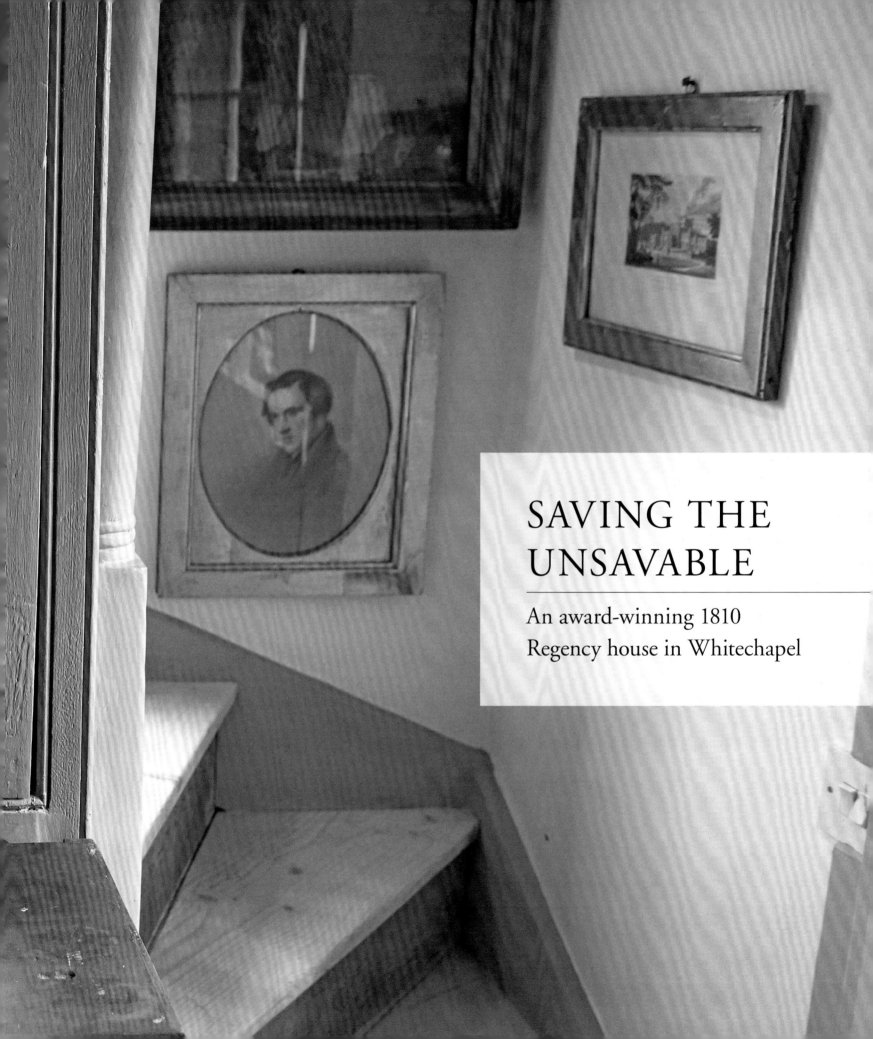

SAVING THE UNSAVABLE

An award-winning 1810
Regency house in Whitechapel

For as long as he can remember, Tim Whittaker has been fascinated by old buildings. His parents were architects, his father collected eighteenth-century furniture. Days spent exploring his childhood home in Sunderland fuelled his interest and knowledge. Aged six, he made scrap albums of local history filled with his photos and drawings.

'My sister sat in the car with a novel,' he grins, fondly remembering weekly cultural outings that were an effective training for his life now, in which he restores endangered old buildings and brings them back into use, mainly as homes, for the Spitalfields Trust. Perhaps because of that informal apprenticeship, his knowledge of old buildings is immense, though worn lightly.

After studying architectural photography he worked for the National Trust as a vernacular buildings surveyor. The Trust was taking stock of all its vernacular holdings and Tim surveyed the Lake District, then Wessex: everyday small buildings, farmhouses and cottages, made not by architects but by builders and masons working with experience and instinct: 'They are what makes a particularly evocative landscape and streetscape.'

He discovered how well traditional buildings adapt to different uses over the centuries. He cites the thirteenth-century merchants' houses in Lacock, Wiltshire, made of timber frames infilled with lath and plaster. Seven hundred years later many are still inhabited, with brick or stone replacing the plaster.

Next, as a National Trust historic buildings representative he looked after the East Midlands, including Calke Abbey, from whose breakfast room comes the paint colour Calke Green. He became interested in original paint surfaces and types, from limewash and distemper to lead paints. 'Which got me interested in decoration and decorative finishes from the seventeenth century onwards. I became aware of the importance of saving such finishes where they survive, so often by accident: on the inside linings of fitted cupboards or inside their doors – old wallpaper, too. And in attics, where the impetus was not redecoration.'

He made hundreds of measured drawings of timber mouldings and learned how they evolved; particularly how

PREVIOUS PAGES A spectacular Giant Triton shell on a case of stuffed waders in front of an old window used as internal glazing.

OPPOSITE LEFT In a small room leading from the back stairs to the front of the house, buttery yellow panelling and a similarly coloured brocaded wing chair have been brought together to make a sunny sitting space.

OPPOSITE RIGHT Back stairs in the rear weatherboard extension are lined in old bead-and-butt matchboarding unified with a slub colour, all overseen by a poetic-looking sixteenth-century gentleman, leaning as casually here as he probably did in life.

BELOW The conservatory, with its plaster casts, sculpture and library, is based on the designs of John Claudius Loudon (1783–1843), a polymath Scottish botanist who designed glasshouses (and introduced the term landscape gardener).

BELOW A perfectly judged display of fine-boned furniture and portraits — particularly a portrait of a lady in a lutestring, or lustering, silk dress, painted around the 1730s — makes this small drawing room a place of consummate charm and elegance.

OPPOSITE Tucked under the eaves with not an inch wasted — a Georgian trick — a romantic galley kitchen lit from a casement window behind the diminutive sink. A flap-down mahogany table is ideal for impromptu cosy breakfasts and lunches.

softwood changed the way mouldings were made and looked when it widely replaced hardwood in the second half of the seventeenth century.

Before that, they were hand-cut with a mouldings plane as an integral part of the furniture. For example, on a sixteenth-century oak chest, a mallet drove the plane along; hard work that partly dictated the form of the profile cut. But once pine was easily available, decorative mouldings were made faster. For a pine architrave, a moulding could be pinned on to a 'plant', or used in many other decorative applications. 'Knocked out, pinned on, filled, and painted,' Tim declares. 'A pine moulding can have several component parts. Paint hides the joins. It was fast, easy and cheap, and allowed classical rooms for the many, so it was democratizing.'

The ease and relative affordability of such decorations meant increasing flamboyance and larger, more complex designs, which corresponded with the rise of Baroque,[1] then Rococo,[2] in Western Europe.

In the late 1990s, Tim was a room steward in his friend Dennis Severs's house, when it was an informal museum. Dennis had heard that the Spitalfields Trust had a job vacancy and suggested Tim apply. He didn't, but a couple of years later the job came up again, when he was doing drawings for a building the Trust was trying to save, and that time he did. 'I was excited to find an organization I felt at one with. Today, well over seventy buildings have passed through its hands, far more than in most similar trusts. It looks for buildings not viable for commercial redevelopment and gives them a fresh use and future, which is usually residential.'

Not just any building, but historic buildings that for whatever reason have decayed to a point where in the past they were often demolished rather than repaired, which still fills Tim with indignation. Fortunately, the pendulum has swung back towards conservation.

'We save the unsavable,' he declares. 'The co-administrator Oliver Leigh-Wood and I work with the clerk of works, Bryan Hole, a former plasterer, who's been there forty years. The Trust is client, contractor, architect, and vendor, so overheads are low, and we use many craftspeople, making employment alongside homes.'

Tim describes his work as romantic. This unusual choice of word encapsulates the ethos of repairing rather than restoring; of keeping the beauty, spirit and existing patina, and of not going an inch further than necessary.

In 2008, the Trust saved ten small early nineteenth-century brick houses in Whitechapel in East London. Built around the time that Tchaikovsky's 1812 Overture was thrilling a changing world, the group belonged to the London Development Agency, which intended to demolish them to make science buildings. Tim says that he was told point blank that 'no one would want to live in them.' On behalf of the Trust, he boldly proposed buying the group for the value the LDA put on it. To do that he would have to find people to restore them in association. The LDA wanted £3,000,000. Tim soon found ten would-be owner occupiers ready to work together to gain a beautiful home.

He describes them as charming little everyday George III townhouses. Leases in the archives of the Royal London Hospital library show that among the original leaseholders there were a doctor, a sea captain, a plumber and a Chelsea Pensioner: 'a real mix of lower-middle class trades'.

They were restored as a harmonious group, with pantile mansards on top and weatherboard additions at the back, using brick, lime, timber and red pantiles. High-walled back gardens were carved from the car park. Craftspeople went from one house to another just as they did in the past, sharing skills, equipment and materials, and learning in the process. 'It was definitely a learning curve,' Tim says. This significant restoration won major awards.

Two years later, in 2009, two houses at the end of the row, which had not been part of the Trust's deal, came up for auction and Tim and his partner, American chef Harvey Cabannis, bought one.

Though similar to the others, their house dates to 1810. A modest three-floor terrace with two rooms per floor, it had original panelling in the ground and first floors, 'but little else'. In the seventies, a roof had been put on, which kept it dry, so although the interiors, unoccupied for fifteen years, were in a mess, they were not rotten. The basement was just six-foot deep, and the back was concrete from the car park.

As with the others, Tim added a tiled mansard. In it he put in a bedroom, bathroom, and a tiny galley kitchen. Into his weatherboarded extension he shoehorned a secondary staircase and a room per floor. He also added a small conservatory in which to display plaster casts. The basement kitchen was lowered and flags found being skipped were wheeled precariously back on a sack-barrow. After digging out the car park hardcore, he built reclaimed brick walls in soft reds, pinks and apricot, with creamy lime mortar and boldly curved ramping details. Espaliered fruit

trees, roses scrambling over an iron arch, box hedges along the walk and traditional planting completed the undertaking.

This house, the last in the terrace (for a long time it was mid-terrace, but the houses beyond were bombed in the Second World War), finishes off the group. Twelve Georgian houses brought back into life. And once their rare and very particular beauty was revealed, they became houses to treasure.

1 An ornate, flamboyant, grandiose style of architecture, design, art and music that obtained from the end of the seventeenth century and ran throughout the eighteenth, principally in Europe.
2 A particular type of ornamentation in architecture, interiors, art and clothing which favoured serpentine lines, scrolling and shell details, and asymmetry. It flourished around the mid-eighteenth century.

LEFT A brown bathroom window is offset by Regency or earlier matchboard turned into a decorative shutter. Exposed to damp, its old lead paint, quickly applied, has weathered to a handsome verdigris colour that would be impossible to copy.

RIGHT A charming view enhances daily life. Here, a kitchen window gives on to the high-walled garden. Reclaimed pinkish-red bricks laid with creamy lime mortar, old terracotta pots, and small plants growing on the outside windowsill all add to the picture.

OVERLEAF The post bed was built around two finely turned walnut end posts, then dressed with various boldly striped tickings (bought in New York) and plain unbleached linen. The lower portrait beside the glazed bedroom door is of an ancestor, painted in 1821.

OPPOSITE ABOVE Beside teddy on the bedroom mantel, an engraving of Wentworth Woodhouse, in Yorkshire. Now owned by a preservation trust, in the eighteenth century It was the largest private house in England and the centre of Whig influence.

OPPOSITE BOTTOM A pleasing old mahogany box of colours, resembling a tea caddy, from T. J. Morris, a Regency brush manufacturer and colourman with premises in Hatton Garden. The full pans of colour have been well used.

BELOW LEFT While some collectors focus on one subject, others enjoy finding visual harmonies between different things, as demonstrated here by the colours and fragility of blown eggshells and the similar properties of translucent porcelain.

BELOW RIGHT A delightful reproduction Regency or early Victorian toy theatre made of cardboard sits atop a bookcase neatly tucked into a wall embrasure. The book spines reveal their owner's interest in architecture and architectural history.

LEFT A large French nineteenth-century museum plaster cast of an anthemion. The Greek term describes a distinctive stylized palmate design much used in architectural friezes, boldly modelled in order to be seen at a distance.

RIGHT This early nineteenth-century plaster bust of a worthy, his hair modishly dressed *à la* Titus, was bought online and arrived painted white to imitate marble. Behind, a rare silk candle fan for a microscope, a nineteenth-century scientific artefact, with its original peacock silk.

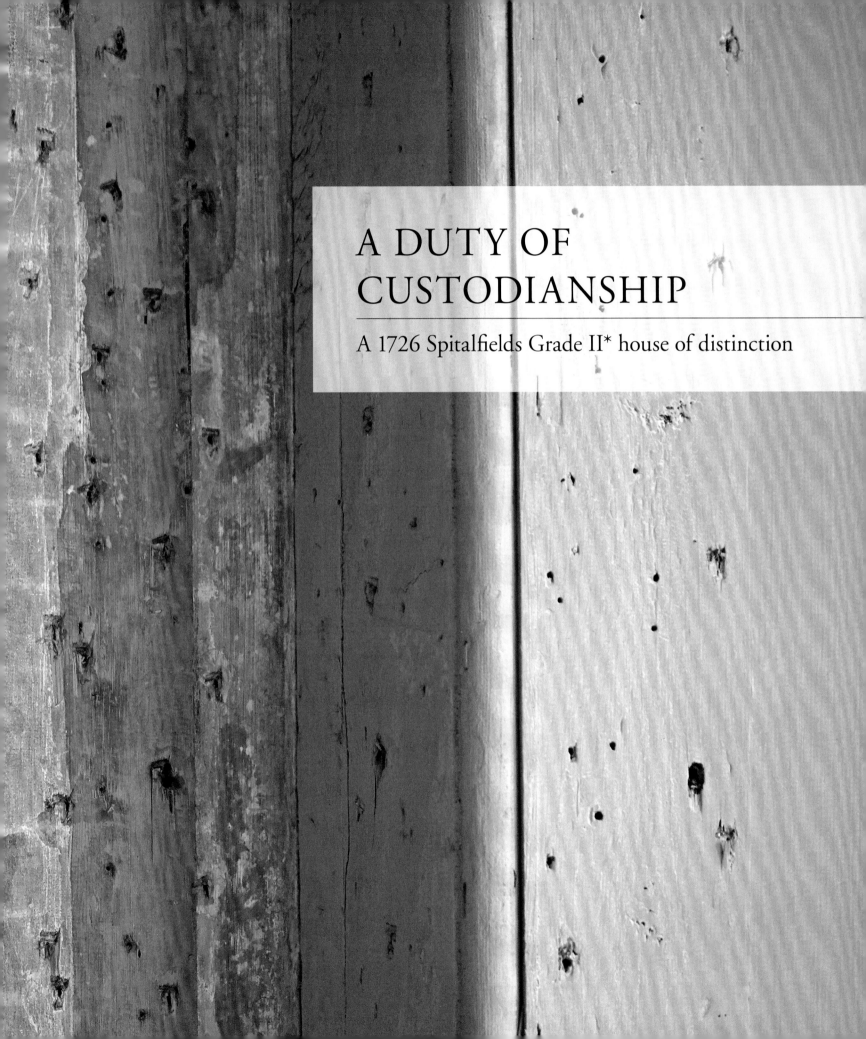

A DUTY OF CUSTODIANSHIP

A 1726 Spitalfields Grade II* house of distinction

In 1967, film star James Mason narrated a 45-minute film called *The London Nobody Knows*. It set the old world against the new one of concrete high-rises where children, he enthused, had somewhere to play other than the doorstep. To make the point he visited Spitalfields, which he called 'mainly for the poor'. Boys brawled along a down-at-heel Fournier Street, now the grandest street in the area. A woman lounged against the fluted door cases of numbers 16 and 18, beside a sign declaring 'Wanted: Machinists'. Mason went into one house in whose yard a Ripper-victim's body was apparently found. As the camera lurched along uneven flagstones it passed a sign for a banana warehouse, a sign common until the fruit-and-vegetable market closed. But Mason did concede that the doors along the street (including their door cases) were among the finest in London.

In just over half a century, what a change has come about.

Unusually, Eleanor Jones's house takes up two building plots. In 1726 they were assigned on a 98-year lease to Marmaduke Smith,[1] a carpenter and successful local property developer, and the first occupant. Smith wanted his big house to be a showcase, 'so he made a point of building it well,' Eleanor says. What he built was five bays wide over three storeys. He did not include a weavers' loft, as if to say there was no intention of conducting *that* trade on his premises. As the plan for the house next door was designed by Nicholas Hawksmoor, the stakes for one-upmanship were high.

The deeply recessed and imposing front door leads into the original wide, panelled, stone-floored hall, which once had symmetrical doors either side. The first thing one sees – and was always meant to see – is a broad mahogany staircase to the first floor, lit by its original landing window with arched top and massive glazing bars. Down the side of this staircase, which is unusually cantilevered from brick internal walls and finished with soaring panelling, the stringers have geometrically patterned walnut parquetry. According to Eleanor this was 'Marmaduke Smith showing off his skills'.

It is thought to be one of the first mahogany staircases in England. The tax on costly imported hardwoods had only been

PREVIOUS PAGES The lines of pinholes in the wood discovered beneath later plasterboard would have been used to affix linen scrim as a base for wallpaper, or, possibly, fabric.

OPPOSITE Gravel walks had already been laid. To these a formal structure of now-mature clipped box and yew was added, interspersed with a gloriously informal planting of splendid tree peonies and roses, both of which flourish here.

BELOW LEFT The attractive bay back of the house shows off the pretensions of its builder, Marmaduke Smith, as do the lion heads supporting the leaded portico to the back door. The pretty twining foliate balconettes render the whole enchanting.

BELOW RIGHT A towering ladder window with thick original glazing bars lights the mahogany and walnut staircase Marmaduke built to demonstrate his skill and wealth. The import tax on costly mahogany had only been lifted the year before.

lifted the previous year, so it was a demonstration of modernity and wealth that no one would misread. Of the princely mahogany of which it is made, Eleanor says, 'I expect he got it off the back of a cart.'

The staircase offers a key to the house. It only rises to the large central first-floor landing, again with original panelling. But Eleanor believes that from here, central double doors probably led to Marmaduke's private suite: bedroom, dressing room and closet, or some such arrangement. Inevitably there have been changes, and a panelled wall now faces the top of the stairs, against which is a good commode, a seventeenth-century mirror carved in the manner of Grinling Gibbons complete with carved corn cobs, and a seventeenth-century clock that keeps fair time.

What makes the house unique is that through a door to the right one enters the servants' wing, which occupies a vertical slice of house. From here stairs rise to the servants' floor, entirely separate from Marmaduke's quarters.

This staircase is bog-standard pine, though painted as imitation mahogany by specialist wood-grainer, Ian Harpur, who also oak-grained the fronts of the former Whitechapel Bell Foundry,[2] and parts of the red bedroom on Smith's floor. The visual trick of faux-mahogany was an easy, quick finish in the eighteenth and nineteenth centuries.

The servants' floor no longer enjoys its original configuration, but one can see where bits of panelling have been economically moved about and in one place a door used as part of a partition. Even in these lesser areas one sees Marmaduke's pride in

the construction of his house, for the floors are white deal, a Scandinavian pine quite different from the pine we know today. Slower growing, so much richer in resin, it was somewhere between hardwood and softwood. Some of the boards are almost fourteen inches wide. It is remarkable that they are this old, yet do not creak, even across such very wide rooms.

'Beneath those particular boards,' Eleanor says, 'some of which show marks of heavy machinery, for like most of the street the house was used in the rag trade during the twentieth century, one beam still has bark on it. It is basically a tree trunk.'

Eleanor bought Marmaduke's house at auction in 2000. Because it had been lived in it wasn't in bad condition. She and her partner, Chris, were intrigued by the servants' side, which they have now absorbed into the rest of the house. It had been

OPPOSITE The servants' side of the house, with plain panelling and the rail clearly visible for the (now removed) stairs, was blocked off. Now this room serves as a breakfast room, in which the formality of a girandole-flanked Milanese eighteenth-century mirror and marbled table is mixed with the cheerful clutter of a busy life.

ABOVE One door leads to what might have been the master's own bedroom, must certainly have been part of his suite; the bed now gloriously hung with new crimson silks, with a cut-down gilded pier mirror over the fireplace. The door beside it links to the separate servants' wing, with plain, drab walls and pine stairs rising to the attic quarters above, where it is unlikely that Marmaduke ever set foot.

blocked off with brick and panelling, and the stairs to the basement boarded over. 'We took the wall panelling off and to our amazement found a door on its hinges in perfect working order,' Eleanor says. That door, the very one that Marmaduke's servants used, now leads into the hall.

It is flashes like these that astonish and enchant owners of old houses. As she first looked around what is now her breakfast room, Eleanor realized that the wooden panelling on the servants' side was much plainer than on the other. Slowly, other clues to past use emerged. A diagonal rail down this partition indicates where a lost section of back stairs apparently ran, then met those down to the basement.

Upstairs, the couple found the first-floor drawing room plastered. There was also a deep cornice, as well as deep skirting boards. 'The plaster didn't feel or look right, and one day I was poking at a loose section with a screwdriver when it fell off to reveal wood.'

Beneath the plaster was eighteenth-century framing, complete with rows of tack-holes where linen scrim had been attached, ready for silk to be put on top. The numerous rows of holes were a clear indication of redecoration.

That framework was painted in greenish drab, a cheap, restful earth colour that would help protect the timber. Eleanor left it and copied it in the breakfast room.

While restoring a seventeenth-century house in Wiltshire, she became interested in the way its builders made the house breathe, and to a degree protect and heal itself. She describes how the internal panels had gaps so that the walls were ventilated and did not become damp, for moisture encourages both rot and insect infestation. On one section of wall, so-called dry rot (now often called brown rot) was developing. This fungus, dreaded by many, will only thrive in certain conditions, and always needs damp to spread. She observed that where the threadlike fungal *hyphae* encountered caustic lime plaster, 'they just died.'

Repairing different houses also taught her to take care when copying details such as cornices, dado rails, and panelling. 'It is important to get it right, to preserve the sense of the actual age of the house. The interesting thing is that you only *really* notice these details if you get them wrong.'

Like so many owners of old houses, Eleanor sees her tenure as guardianship rather than ownership; one of thoughtful repair rather than heavy-handed restoration. She calls it 'a duty of custodianship.'

To that end, in case a future owner wants to reinstate it, she stores a door that once led to Marmaduke Smith's business room at the front of the house. The room is now a comfortable snug, and it's easy to imagine him there, a beady eye on the comings and goings along his street.

1 'The Wood-Mitchell estate: Fournier Street', in *Survey of London: Volume 27, Spitalfields and Mile End New Town*, ed. F. H. W. Sheppard (London, 1957), pp. 199-225. British History Online.

2 The medieval Whitechapel Bell Foundry sited on New Road cast Big Ben and America's Liberty Bell but its world-famous premises were sold in 2017.

OPPOSITE Gilded eighteenth-century girandoles grace the wall, which is just as it was when discovered beneath plasterboard, scarred by marks of successive wallpaper or silk hangs. The original cheap earth green, never intended to be seen, was left.

RIGHT The difference between silk and synthetic fabrics is that even when silk begins to rot and split from wear and long exposure to sunlight, it is still beautiful and worth keeping. This is especially true of hand-woven, brocaded and tuft-trimmed silk such as is used here.

BELOW The double drawing room doors were copied from those on the floor below, as the originals were lost. They replace a modern plasterboard wall that ran right across. In the corner, a gleaming Korean hardwood chest makes a stand for two Delft plates.

LEFT With formality appropriate to a drawing room a gilded Italian canapé from about 1830 on turned walnut legs, upholstered in grey-green silk brocade, sits against a French *verdure* tapestry, featuring trees and woodland, perhaps made to convey a sense of *rus in urbe*.

RIGHT What better place for an ambitious businessman such as Marmaduke Smith to have a vantage point than here on the first floor, where he could gaze at the comings and goings of the street? (As he no doubt also did from the business room below – but that was more public.)

LEFT An unusual and charming original curved shutter-bar holds the lower set of internal shutters together for privacy, while gently echoing the curve of the bay window into which it is set.

BELOW Carpentry and joinery skills are on display throughout this house, which once acted as a business calling card. The impressive curved window bays with their raised-field panelled recesses make a glamorous finale to the large dining room.

OPPOSITE The dining room's mid-grey-blue was specially mixed. Its dignified hue is a good foil for the rich warmth of the vast mahogany dining table and Georgian chairs from three sets, one set embellished with admirable foliate parquetry.

A CONNECTION WITH THE PAST

The 1725 house that began a movement in 1976

Landscape gardener Paul Gazerwitz and his partner Andrew Brader, along with Molly and Ted, their Burmese cats, live in one of a pair of narrow and rare weavers' houses. Rare because each was built with an unusual two-storey weavers' loft and an elegant showroom on the ground floor: in other words, designed as factories with retail outlets – but around 1725. Yet, despite their rarity, 250 years later, in 1977, Paul's house had just had its top knocked off by a demolition crew. One more day and the rest of this unique house would have thundered into the dust.

The method used was a particularly egregious one known as bookending, in which terrace houses are knocked down one by one, leaving the exposed ones propped and vulnerable, thus reinforcing the argument that the destruction should continue. This pair were the next for the chop. Photographs show the twin houses externally propped up with great wooden spars and the roof of Paul's gone, though its rib-like joists remained, incised with Roman numerals to aid construction. The upper windows had been smashed. To the untrained eye the pair looked irredeemable. To the trained eye they were historic catnip. And so it was these two houses that the Spitalfields Trust squatted (see page 9), which emergency action by the group of romantic academics and idealists made history.

The houses were built between 1725 and 1727, after Sir Isaac Tillard granted a 61-year lease to Thomas Bunce.

According to the Survey of London, both were built by March 1726 or 1727 and Bunce assigned mortgages at £250 and £337 respectively to a Spitalfields weaver,[1] perhaps the person who connected them with a second-floor veranda, which on Paul's side is now a small bathroom with two beautiful paint-scraped doors, one formerly external.

Before Paul bought his house in 2003 it had been through a great deal. In the Second World War the basement was an ad hoc bomb shelter. Its floor, once flagged or tiled, had been replaced by concrete and the window embrasures had been filled in with concrete blocks. There was a concrete pillar in the middle of what is now the kitchen.

PREVIOUS PAGES A rim-lock with mismatched keep on the site of a former lock; all scraped, leaving a record of time.

OPPOSITE Ted, a young black Bombay, keeps watch out of a first-floor window, which still has its original shutters and panelling. The old white on the walls has been there for at least fifty years. This house retains a great deal of historic detail.

BELOW LEFT As in John's house (see page 87), a small corner sink on the upper stairs — this one very plain — served the several occupants. At one time a coal miner lived here and would have had to wash in this sink. There was no indoors lavatory or bath.

BELOW RIGHT The house was built as one of a pair with the one next door, connecting via a small balcony. After 1977 when the houses were saved from demolition and separated, the balcony, closed off from next door, was turned into a modest bathroom.

In the middle of the century the house was owned by a moneylender, who hung fifties wallpaper, some of which Paul uncovered. This landlord possessed the only car and fridge in the street, for the area was a slum. There was one small shared sink on the stairs, which is still there, and an outside privy. Life must have been hard for the tenants.

When the houses were saved and repaired in the seventies it was on a tight budget. Paul's future home got a new roof and a rudimentary kitchen in what is now his bedroom, but he says there wasn't enough money to tackle the basement.

A couple bought the houses and continued their repair, but they too left the hellhole of a basement alone. Then the joined pair was split back into two.

Living nearby, Paul was aware of them, and when one came up for sale he bought it. 'I knew it was very original. There were original timber cornices in most rooms. There is a distinct local vocabulary for these mouldings, which were all done by the same carpenters and builders who went from house to house, running them out.'

He found almost all the panelling *in situ*: slender partition walls; imposing three-quarter panelling along the hall's spine wall; and built-in cupboards, including full-height corner cupboards and display cupboards. The horrible basement even had the original large timber fire surround. All the floorboards were intact too, narrower on the highest floors.

In the back ground-floor room an unusual flush timber fire surround to the canted fireplace had been skipped, possibly by

OPPOSITE Three-quarter-height panelling in the hall has been patiently scraped to reveal various layers of paint in early colours made of earth pigments from yellow ochre to green earth. The process is painstakingly slow but gives a rewarding result.

RIGHT The dividing door between front and back rooms on the ground floor is quite austere, as is the nearby panelling, which is plain and square-cut. The black reeded ball rim knobs were in the house and are probably Regency.

BELOW RIGHT Unexpected glimpses provide joy in these old houses, such as a view from the kitchen up to the hall, showing the curved lime-plaster soffit under the stairs, and ochre dragging done by Jocasta Innes (1934–2013, author of the influential *Paint Magic*).

OPPOSITE TOP In the corner of the 'wet' kitchen at the front of the house was a shallow sink, hollowed out from a slab of limestone, which has been kept.

OPPOSITE BOTTOM This rare timber fire surround has been kept, with some repairs. Many flags had been moved to the yard. Brought back in, they were laid on sand in the traditional way. The walls are limewashed, knocked back with a dab of raw umber.

BELOW Reopened, restored windows and an original alcove cupboard door, its yellow ochre partly scraped, make a genial background for some undecorated nineteenth-century Lambethware jugs, which complement the jars on the mantelpiece.

the demolition crew. Remarkably, Spitalfields Trust founder Dan Cruickshank spotted it, broken in pieces. He fished the bits out and kept them until they could be reinstated.

'I felt an immediate connection with this house,' Paul says. 'I knew everything was still there beneath the modern paint, which was exciting. All the little bolts and hinges, too. From all those things you get a sense of how people lived in the eighteenth century.'

He even found two large hooks either side of the back door, into which the owners set a timber length at night – a rudimentary London bar.

He immediately stripped the concrete out of the basement. New windows with thick glazing bars were made to match those in neighbouring houses. Once the floor was back to dirt, he laid three-inch flags straight on sand in the traditional manner. He found half in the back yard; the rest were reclaimed. The original limestone sink was still in the corner, very shallow, mercifully not broken, hollowed from one flagstone, above what might be a small bread oven.

Next he repaired the huge fire surround. On the window wall he designed a simple kitchen, made by a local carpenter. Plain iron butterfly hinges, though new, are like eighteenth-century ones.

Once the walls had been lime-plastered he painted them with three coats of limewash mixed in a bucket, its bright white knocked back with a dab of raw umber.

Paul then spent years 'dry-scraping' away layers of modern paint throughout the house, using chemical stripper to loosen the top layer, then scraping by hand to reveal early layers, wearing gloves and a mask as a precaution against lead. One cannot rush such work, and part of it is to enjoy the panoramic kaleidoscope of colours as you cut through layers. In places he left an array of colours in order to savour their particular and historic beauty.

Whereas the principal rooms of many eighteenth-century houses are on the first floor, here the ground-floor showroom was more important. The ceilings are the highest in the house. A large box cornice runs around the top of full-height panelling, made from three sections joined together.

The front room had been painted in imitation of lead white by the previous owners and Paul kept it like that. But he stripped the panelling in the back room down to its earliest layer, ochre.

This small room, with its clear light and intact walls and cornice – and its reinstated fire surround – makes an ideal foil for well-chosen modern furniture as well as for that of the eighteenth century. A small mid-twentieth-century two-seater settle is a perfect height against the chair-rail. Paul took a long time choosing it.

'I grew up in America and these things speak to me. It is all about good design and proportion.'

He re-covered an eighteenth-century horsehair sofa with eighteenth- or early nineteenth-century crimson silk velvet bought from a specialist dealer. This exquisite and costly fabric had already been used as curtains and he recut it. It is a match for the worn-out velvet that previously covered the sofa, pieces of which he kept.

Paul knows how to paint and how to mix paint. He wanted to preserve the fabric of the house where he found or uncovered it very much as it had been. The lives of its former owners and the sense and feeling of those lives are clearly important to him. He senses them in every original part of the house, whether in the colours of the walls, or old hooks and hinges and other vestigial traces, some of which were there to see, some of which he discovered bit by bit, forming a close bond with the building. But he expresses a note of caution, too: 'These houses need a strong personality to wrestle with them, but I do it out of joy, because I find them inexpressibly beautiful.'

1 'The St. John and Tillard estate: Elder Street', in *Survey of London: Volume 27, Spitalfields and Mile End New Town*, ed. F. H. W. Sheppard (London, 1957), pp. 81–87. British History Online.

OPPOSITE, FAR LEFT, ABOVE
& BELOW The street floor was
the showroom for the silk
manufactory on the top two
floors, so – unusually – it had
the highest ceiling. It also had
large, elegant box cornices,
which remain. All these walls
have been taken right back
to their original colour, then
waxed, bringing this pair of
rooms very close to how
they began.

OPPOSITE, LEFT Dan
Cruickshank found the fire
surround to the canted chimney
In the smaller back room on
a skip, broken in two, and
stored it. The charming room is
furnished with mid-twentieth-
century modern furniture,
which suits the scale and the
dado height.

RIGHT, ABOVE A landscape
artist's eye finds colours and
shapes in harmony with the
exquisite original proportions
and colours of this small
chamber, bridging the
centuries. The full-height corner
cupboard balances the canted
chimney breast.

RIGHT, BELOW Paul owns a
Georgian sofa uphostered in
eighteenth-century silk, but
for here he chose a 1960 Eero
Saarinen two-seater sofa whose
overall diminutive size is a
perfect fit against the height
of the chair-rail. It looks very
happy next to a Georgian
tilt-top table.

LEFT A Rococoesque nineteenth-century French bed adorns the bedroom. A former kitchen cupboard was taken apart ('turned into flatpack') to get it upstairs. The cat, drawn in 1945, is by the Danish Kay Christensen (1899–1981), Edvard Munch's pupil.

RIGHT Leaving well alone often offers rewards, as here, where a Bakelite dolly switch with surface cable sits on scraped wood next to the evidence of an earlier site, all in visual harmony with a 1964 oil painting by Hugh Walker of the Maltings, Sawbridgeworth.

THE SMALLEST HOUSE
IN THE STREET

One-room-per-floor in a 1727 house in Spitalfields

'If I like it, it's here,' announces Basil Comely, former Editor of BBC Arts London: 'Georgian tat, Victorian tat, Edwardian tat. I only have bric-a-brac. Some people furnish as if their house were Holkham or Houghton Hall.[1] But this is a humble house, although some of the mouldings are quite grand.'

Basil's house is full of pictures and artefacts picked up from junk shops over the years – rarely from auctions. He spurns the term collector for himself, saying that his tastes change.

There are a bewildering number of framed prints; numerous taxidermy specimens, some under glass but others lolling or looming unexpectedly, even from the top of cupboards; and porcelain, which is almost all skilfully mended. One's attention constantly shifts here and there, from a stuffed magpie flying high from the hall ceiling to the mixed blue-and-white porcelain serried on the egg-yolk yellow kitchen dresser, to a dining room table covered with things being sorted out prior to repainting the room, to jugs, mugs, porcelain cats or dogs and a plastic raven, to old glass bottles jostling shoulder-to-shoulder on windowsills. A magpie himself, Basil buys whatever catches his eye. And every item is somehow perfectly, happily displayed in this strongly coloured house, whose walls range from deep brown on the stairs to the kitchen's yellow, Calke Green in the study and whited cobalt blue in the one modest bathroom. 'Nothing ruins a Georgian house like too many bathrooms,' he declares.

There are also inherited family things, none of great intrinsic value but each of irreplaceable sentimental worth. Stories are important to this born raconteur: 'Many of these things tell a story. I have my great-great-uncle Colonel Graves's sword from

PREVIOUS PAGES Against the leaf-green-painted original plaster rests a big, splendid ammonite fossil bought in Lyme Regis.

OPPOSITE Cheery, glossy egg-yolk yellow lights the basement kitchen and makes a good background for a varied collection of china from eighteenth-century plates to amusing modern mugs. Many pieces have intriguing tales to tell. The ceiling is Victorian, along with the floor tiles and bible chairs, while the table was made from timber salvaged from Brighton's celebrated West Pier.

RIGHT 'I went big on taxidermy when I moved in. If I had known that the Spitalfields moth population was a plague, I might not have bought quite so much.' Nevertheless, six grouped cased birds, so far untroubled, look very fine in the first-floor sitting room.

BELOW The sitting room – grained and cobwebbed all over with a gun – was once a set for Scrooge's counting house in a TV advert, The cobwebs have gone but the colour remains, a fitting background for prints and stuffed animals.

LEFT On the warm chocolate-brown woodwork of the hall and stairs, every inch is used for (often witty) display. Miniature diecast painted cars and trucks from the 1950s drive along the moulding; paintings above and below provide hard shoulders.

BELOW Every floor has a round 'fish-eye' mirror, the sort painted by Van Eyck, all from junk shops: 'They are useless for looking at yourself in but they do attractive things to a room.' Set in an angle of the staircase this one demonstrates the principle well.

OPPOSITE, LEFT Prints and engravings, architectural, topographical and figurative, wait in stacked huddles on the stairs to be delicately attached to the surrounding walls – should an unoccupied space ever emerge.

OPPOSITE, RIGHT Coloured Georgian engravings at the foot of the stairs mock human foibles and life itself, while providing company for an ancestor's warming pan (sometimes mistaken for a bedpan, sometimes for an unstrung banjo).

the Indian Army; Grandpa Christopher Comely's bayonet from the First World War; and my grandmother's family's bedwarmer, which people mistake for a bedpan.' Next to two framed Victorian embroideries in the hall ticks an Edwardian wall clock that once hung above his grandmother's oven, and bears scorch marks to prove it. 'Just looking at it, I am back in Granny's cottage,' he says.

Mason Jonathan Beaumont built the tall narrow house as one of a pair under a 61-year lease granted in 1727. Five years after completion the lease was assigned to a Whitechapel printer who apparently did good business, for he had other properties in the area.[2]

With its simple design of five square rooms stacked like children's building blocks, one corner cut out of each in order to insert the tall, twisting staircase, this house is not for those who espouse living on one floor. 'Fifty-two stairs up to bed,' Basil says with relish. With its small grate and casement window, the attic bedroom is a world away from the rush of the cobbled street below. The old deal staircase, its softly shining treads smoothly dipped by the tender and not so tender rub of passing feet over centuries, also provides wall space for a packed array of prints. Basil caught the print-buying bug as a child in Gloucestershire, scouring a local junk yard at the weekend with his aunt. Many other framed prints, as yet unhung, stand stacked throughout the house, their faces to the wall.

With its blade-like post around which the stairs seem almost visibly to rotate, the staircase exemplifies Georgian economy. But one wonders how skirted servants passed their employers without a close brush of fabric, or perhaps an occasional unwanted fumble.

According to Basil, before he arrived in 2001 his house had already had hundreds of inhabitants, some documented. It previously belonged to radical left-wing historian Raphael Samuel and his wife, scholar Alison Light. Raised a Communist, Raphael bought the house in the early sixties and lived there until his death in 1996. In 1994, he published the first volume of his great work, *Theatres of Memory*. After his death, Raphael's widow decided to sell.

Basil had been living in 'a beautiful small Victorian house in Camberwell, in the mode of the TV show *Coronation Street*', when his friend Dan Cruickshank mentioned a Georgian house for sale. 'If truth be told, my taste is more Victorian Gothic, and this street seemed very grown up. My Camberwell house had more rooms but I didn't use them all, whereas here I use all five rooms every day.

'For a while I was slightly overawed at owning a fragile house. The day after I moved in the bathroom ceiling fell down. If you put in a picture hook on the first floor something will fall off on the second, and there is a dent in the ceiling plaster of the stairwell where a piano was stuck for three days. If you do one thing, you uncover another that needs doing.

'But I have always been determined to decorate the house myself. It doesn't matter that there are paint dribbles. I know every contour. I love the bow of the kitchen ceiling beneath its probably Victorian tongue-and-groove covering. At first, I used an eighteenth-century colour palette, but I'm now doing a Soanian range, stretching to the 1860s.

'These houses breathe. I use oil paint on wood, and water-based paint on plaster.' And because they have no foundations bar a few courses of brick, Basil explains, the house moves, so

that a window can stick for five years and suddenly move freely again. It also sometimes groans unexpectedly.

A modest, conscientious conservationist, he has done very little, and that only when absolutely necessary. When he had to replace two window panes that shattered when a sash window slipped, he had the replacement glass specially blown.

When he moved in, there was a simple bathroom in the back corner of the kitchen, on top of the small red terracotta tiles laid by Raphael Samuel, who had shared a job lot of reclaimed tiles with a neighbour. This rather ad hoc arrangement only contained a sink and a bath. In the yard outside was the cramped sixties khazi the Samuels used. And for the first eighteen months Basil dutifully went outside, even in snow, until eventually the local joiner set a panelled partition wall across the back section of his study, copying mouldings, just

OPPOSITE & ABOVE LEFT A library fills two walls of the second-floor study. The attractive bookcase began as shelving in an old-fashioned chemist's.

ABOVE RIGHT The L-shaped room had a pine partition put across the smaller back part, just the way it would have been done when the house was first built, in this case in order to make the only bathroom in the house – replacing a khazi in the yard, which was freezing in winter.

BELOW A group of blue-green glass bottles like misty semiprecious jewels on the bathroom windowsill. Mainly nineteenth or early twentieth century, some were moulded with the unambiguous word POISON in thankfully large letters.

OPPOSITE, LEFT The narrow, deep bath is said to have come from a house lived in by the writer D.H. Lawrence and his wife, Frieda, either or both of whom may have used it. Miraculously it was got up the stairs, and it was re-enamelled for decades more of useful service.

OPPOSITE, RIGHT Outside the blue ledge-and-brace back door, the small, high-walled yard in which white pelargoniums and acanthus bask.

as it would have been done centuries ago. This divided off a small room to accommodate a narrow standing bath and a thunderous old toilet. The secondhand bath Basil bought and resurfaced is very slim in the hip and was apparently once used by D.H. Lawrence.

Freed of its khazi, the pocket-handkerchief-sized, high-walled yard has become a haven for hostas, acanthus, and white pelargoniums that soak up the only bit of sun when it loiters, briefly, near the back door. And the kitchen has been returned to its original shape.

Basil's way of life would have struck a chord with earlier inhabitants, who included a maker of so-called Leghorn, or

Livorno, straw hats, which add a pastoral touch to mid-eighteenth-century paintings.[3] He says his house has not been 'architected' to look old. Rather, it is authentically old: 'This one has all the marks, the scars and distress of the decades. You can still see that through the paint.'

He believes that the subdued light, which he calls gloom, and the quietness of his house and others like it encourage a sense of purpose and concentration. Not only for humans but also for moths: 'Perhaps if I had known that the Spitalfields moth population was a plague,' he says, characteristically deadpan, 'I might not have bought quite so much taxidermy.'

1 Holkham Hall is an imposing eighteenth-century Palladian manor in Norfolk, built by Thomas Coke, first Earl of Leicester, 1734–1764, and still the seat of the Earls of Leicester. Houghton Hall, also in Norfolk, was built in the 1720s by Britain's first prime minister, Thomas Walpole. It was designed by Colen Campbell, with interiors by William Kent. Both houses are spectacular examples of English Palladianism.

2 'The St. John and Tillard estate: Elder Street', in *Survey of London: Volume 27, Spitalfields and Mile End New Town*, ed. F. H. W. Sheppard (London, 1957), pp. 81–87. British History Online.

3 A fine example of a plaited straw Leghorn hat, traditionally wide-brimmed and shallow-crowned, is worn by Mrs Andrews in *Mr and Mrs Andrews*, 1748–1750, by Gainsborough, in the National Gallery, London.

BELOW Light plays across the mercury glass of a gilded mirror on an alcove cupboard in the dining room, painted a faded Venetian red with one panel left the previous colour. A Victorian painting of a dog filching a man's supper adds a wry touch.

OPPOSITE With crisp dentil detail and lobate shelves, its matchboard lining painted a good blue, a deal corner cupboard with a missing door makes a pleasing and useful display cabinet for lustreware, Staffordshire figures, and even a discarded glass.

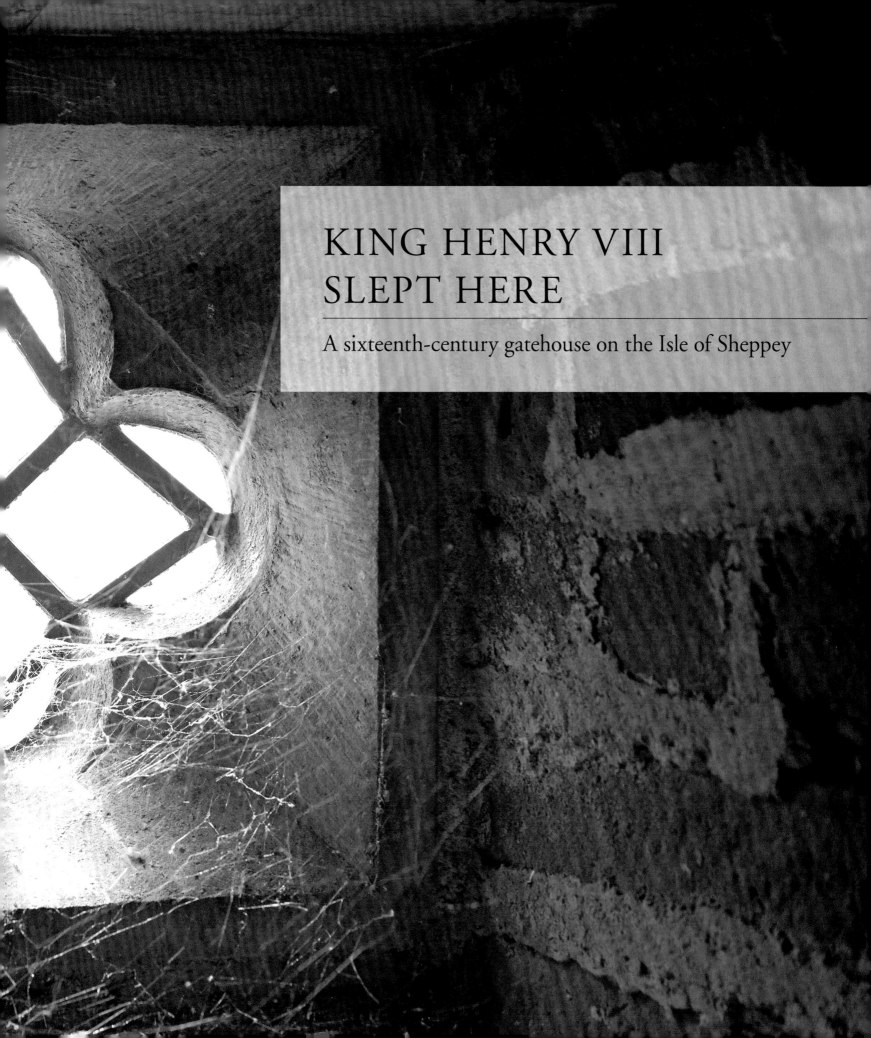

KING HENRY VIII
SLEPT HERE

A sixteenth-century gatehouse on the Isle of Sheppey

Across the wind-whipped Isle of Sheppey in Kent, on 9 October 1532, jangled the caparison bells and spurs of a retinue of hundreds, as King Henry VIII and Anne Boleyn, his soon-to-be second wife, rode towards a boat to France for a meeting with King Francis I of France. This dramatic procession followed a two-day stay at Shurland Hall, a new manor house in the great enclosed estate of Sir Thomas Cheyney, or Cheyne, who built it. Islanders and sheep scattered along the route – the sheep after which Sheppey is named – must have been dazzled by Anne, glittering in Queen Katherine's jewellery, some of which Henry had already given her. The couple would marry in secret a month later, and officially two months after that. Cheyney was her distant relation by marriage. He lavished money on the royal visit, an exceptional honour, and would eventually hold an extraordinary array of offices including those of Treasurer of the Royal Household, Knight of the Garter, Warden of the Cinque Ports, and Lord Lieutenant of Kent.[1] Yet within a century, the estate was an Elizabethan garrison; it then fell into disrepair and continued to decline. By the mid twentieth century, all that was left of the house that Thomas had so proudly built was the stone front porch and a partial wall. But its grand gatehouse still stood, though with no roof and no windows; long stretches of the enclosing walls remained too. A *memento mori* if there ever was one: the deer enclosure empty, the industrious small buildings gone.

In 2006, the Spitalfields Trust took on the repair of Shurland Hall, before the project became unfeasible. This was a labour of love that might easily have become a folly, for the undertaking was immense. Set in seven acres, Shurland is a designated

Ancient Monument, and Grade II* listed. By then the name Shurland Hall had been transferred to the dilapidated, roofless gatehouse, for the main house was beyond repair.

Built of warm red brick partly diapered with grey, set on a ragstone base, with majestic octagonal ragstone-quoined red-brick castellated turrets, the wide gatehouse, despite being only one room thick, was once as magnificent as a peacock fanning its tail. After five years of continual restoration using traditional skills and materials it was returned to something very like its original appearance. As a final flourish, tall red twisting Tudor chimneys were rebuilt by a master bricklayer. Inside, a wooden newel staircase was built in one turret up to the roof, and at one end an eighteenth-century staircase from a demolished house in Hatton Garden was inserted.[2]

PREVIOUS PAGES A small quatrefoil window in one of the gatehouse turrets, beautiful as well as functional.

OPPOSITE & BELOW The walls surrounding the seven acres of Shurland Hall, the name now given to the gatehouse of the former hall, are a national monument. The principal remnant of the original house is its stone porch, through which sheep sometimes wander.

By 2011 all the major work had been done, under the eye of Historic England. That work was extensive. It included the structural rebuilding of sections of the gatehouse and an entire new roof. Terracotta and timber floors were laid; leaded mullion windows painstakingly made to the front, conjuring up the past in every tiny flashing pane; the great timber surround to the nailed oak portal was re-carved; stone fireplace surrounds restored. In places, inventive reuse of reclaimed church panelling and joinery created a vestibule for the Great Hall and dado panelling in the former snug guardroom to one side of the entrance. The addition of an orangery completed the damaged end of one flank, creating a welcome family room, sunlit from three sides.

But smaller works were still required. Beyond a compact new orchard of young apple trees and oaks lining the drive, the surrounding land needed planting, and the house needed further wiring and plumbing, along with decorating and furnishing. It needs very special people to take on a house like this, so full of history: they must be mindful of the weight of the past and the gravity of custodianship embedded in its every flagstone, ragstone, and quoin. Such a mantle cannot be worn lightly. In 2012, the Trust found the right owner-custodians in Daniel and Suzanne O'Donoghue, who run a small champagne import business from the Hall, along with caring for their house and land.

OPPOSITE A view of the back of the red-brick-and-ragstone gatehouse from the porch of the old house shows the magnificent Tudor chimneys, completely rebuilt by a master bricklayer during the Spitalfields Trust's complex restoration project under the eagle eye of Historic England.

BELOW LEFT Without roof or windows, the hall was in a parlous state. During the lengthy rebuild and restoration these fine mullioned leaded windows were installed, twinkling and glittering as they once would have done.

BELOW RIGHT A detail of the restored massive door to the gatehouse, which would have presented a line of defence had the property ever come under attack. It is through this historic portal that Henry VIII entered with his bride-to-be, Anne Boleyn.

LEFT The Great Hall of the one-room-thick gatehouse is spectacular. The stone fire surround (not shown) was found in the grounds. A church vestibule now makes a fitting vestibule to the eating room, complete with its Tudor table and a Charles II court cupboard.

OPPOSITE Bright, clear Yeabridge green walls make a nice contrast with dark oak furniture. Two as yet unhung corbels of painted plaster-on-wood sixteenth-century courtly boys flank a carved oak eighteenth-century money box, on an unassociated bookcase.

The couple met at university in Sheffield, and almost immediately began a life of antiquing. Their first purchase was a Victorian wheelchair, a quirky buy that mystified their friends. A natural step from buying old furniture was to renovate dilapidated old buildings. They furnished them with brown furniture, often cheaper than modern equivalents, and particularly liked massy seventeenth-century pieces. They also bought portraits at auction or wherever else they spotted them. In 1990, the couple restored Woodcroft Castle near Peterborough, then Elizabethan Hautbois Castle in Norwich, built in 1553. This prepared them perfectly to adopt Shurland.

They are passionate about their new home and caring for it properly. At first there was only one power point, so at breakfast the toaster and the kettle had to take turns. The Trust had in storage an oak kitchen from another property it was restoring and offered it to them. Painted mid-grey by Suzanne, it graces the spacious kitchen. This light, large shuttered room, warmly tiled, is full of old dressers and hanging cupboards. Throughout the house the couple has used much of the seventeenth-century furniture that Dan favours, along with a Tudor stretcher table in the Great Hall, and a gigantic gleaming nineteenth-century table that seats twenty in the dining room. This table was donated by the Trust because it was too big to move. The chairs are mismatched, which doesn't matter a bit. On the contrary, such pleasing jolts are a reminder that this is a home, not a museum.

Portraits of women adorn one room and men the other. Not rare, chosen for character as much as beauty, some of them are real battleaxes, but they add huge and iconoclastic charm.

A large framed poster of Anne Boleyn that the children gave Suzanne is here, too, masquerading as a painting, just as Anne perhaps once masqueraded as a queen.

Suzanne, who masterminds the interiors, had shutters made rather than curtains, for the windows are large and the fabric yardage would have been immense, but she did add curtains here and there, sensibly made from new tapestry or brocade in old designs, rather than using fragile antique textiles. The floorboards are washed with a soapy solution, allowing them

to slowly build up a gentle finish, a bit like liming, rather than oiling or polishing them.

The couple have worked very hard outside, too. Fruit bushes are protected in their own enclosure, while three laying hens with fluffy brown trousers occupy another section. Strictly for eggs, these delightful creatures will never be eaten. Loosely strewn wild-flower beds; shrub and climbing roses; imperial poppies and other arrangements of flowers soften and enhance the glowing brickwork.

OPPOSITE Tallulah the Bengal relaxes on a chaise surrounded by an intriguing group of 'women in bonnets' and a framed poster of Anne Boleyn. The long flame mahogany table came from the Bishop's Palace in Fulham and sits on soap-washed boards.

ABOVE When the couple moved in, the sunny kitchen had one tap and one socket. Now it is the hub of the home, with salvaged cupboards painted grey, and a delightful dresser designed to house chickens in its lower section.

LEFT A view through an original arched doorway from the guardroom to the entry hall, towards two 1815 Regency overmantel mirrors and a crossed toy sword and shield (which a now-elderly local man remembers playing with in the ruins of Shurland Hall when he was a boy).

OPPOSITE Today the guardroom is a comfortable room in the gatehouse's centre; but once, visitors had to pass it successfully to go on to the great house beyond, aware of bristling arms to one side. Its rope settle, now with a wooden seat, still has its rope holes.

Dan strims and mows, and in due course the long barn, surrounded by attractive informal planting, will be used for wedding receptions.

Taking on a project like this is completely unlike anything else. It creates its own way and rhythm of life and certainly wouldn't suit everyone, for it makes many demands. But in their sympathetic furnishing of the long, large rooms, with, in particular, generally not grand wooden furniture that has already lived alongside humans for a few hundred years; and by not over-furnishing, not carpeting, not fussing, this couple are keeping a magnificent building that was so nearly lost to the nation in very good order. Indeed, as well as enjoying it, which is crucial, they are enhancing it. This is what the business of living in and caring for old buildings is all about.

And who knows what king or queen, and what retinue jangling bells, may one day yet again pass through this gatehouse set high on the shoreland overlooking the sea?

1 Sheila M Judge, *The Isle of Sheppey*, Rochester Press, 1983, p.36.
2 Spitalfields Trust: www.spitalfieldstrust.com/project/new-shurland-hall-eastchurch-isle-of-sheppey-kent/

BELOW LEFT Details such as the small stone Tudor doorway into an ensuite bathroom make Shurland unique. Its restoration trod a successful path between retaining as much historic material as possible, yet making a realistically habitable home.

BELOW RIGHT A light-hearted group: a pair of nineteenth-century Staffordshire spaniels flank a pretty polychrome jug on a well proportioned mahogany commode. Mixing furniture periods and decorative styles in a home is fun and rewarding.

LEFT Imagine who looked through this door before: time is ever present, and such games continue with the central table, a seventeenth-century tilt table, later re-carved in Arts and Crafts style – an oblique parallel with the story of Shurland itself.

OPPOSITE The walls show all the history of this place, from the small handmade red bricks (which have not been repointed), stylishly diapered in black, to the ragstone base on which the bricks were laid, and an original, salt-wind-worn stone window surround.

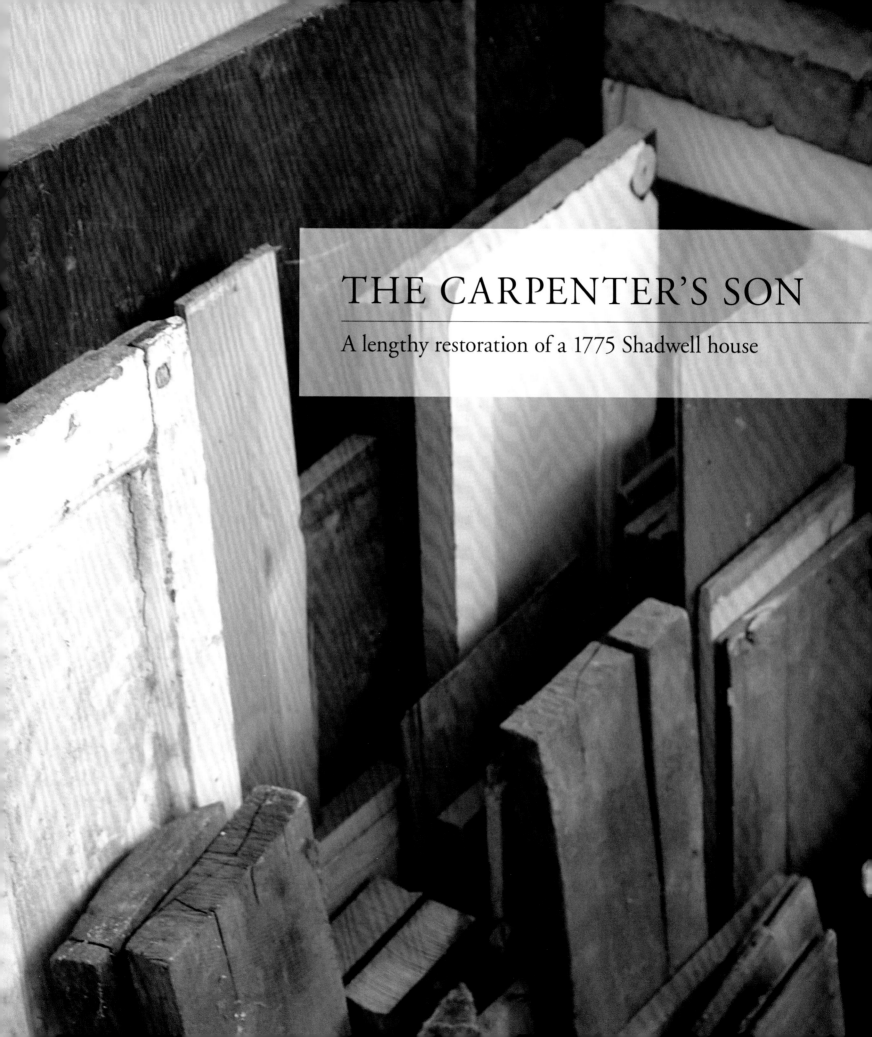

THE CARPENTER'S SON

A lengthy restoration of a 1775 Shadwell house

Some of us store up early experiences as grist for a future mill. During his South London childhood, Dan Lucas watched his father, a carpenter, work. Dan was only allowed to make measurements and mark timber: 'Measure twice, cut once,' was his father's wise maxim. But, like any gung-ho child, Dan longed to try a saw, and around eight or nine was allowed to. It marked the precocious beginnings of a skill that would prove very useful later. A love of old furniture developed into rescuing occasional doors or fire surrounds from skips. When his family moved to an Edwardian house, a buried hoard of broken encaustic tiles turned up in the back garden. He tried to reassemble the patterns. While not an unqualified success, it was the ideal jigsaw puzzle for a burgeoning restorer who, in his own words, 'can't abide waste'.

Around 2007, renting in east London, he began looking for a house to repair and restore. In 2010, he found one.

When it was built, in 1775, the four-storey terrace house in Shadwell was part of new development on recent pastureland.[1] Perhaps a sea captain's house, for the docks and Tower Bridge are within walking distance, it had high ceilings and stylish big windows. There was a generous divided ground floor and fine first floor for entertaining, similarly divided. A small back yard held a cesspit.

But Shadwell declined. In the 1851 census, sixteen people were noted living there: four distinct families, and possibly one or two undocumented clerks or journeymen. Crime, drugs and prostitution were prevalent and the area continued to slide.

In the early 1970s, two young actors bought the house for £3,000 in cash from a man they'd met in a working men's club who wanted to move to a two-bedroom flat in Dagenham with an indoor bathroom. Dan recounts the story with relish. At that time the Shadwell house was in bad condition, carved into bedsits with a sink in each room, and what Dan calls a bothy in the back yard. On which fertile spot the couple soon planted a camellia. Now a spectacular tree, it demonstrates the benefit of recycling organic material.

Fortunately, because the pair were artists and not well off, they did little to their new home besides necessary repairs. The gutter of the butterfly roof had failed, causing water damage, and the building was gently sinking in the middle. Floorboards were damaged too, and the first-floor panelling had rotted, so they removed it. What decorating they did was done with sympathy. They put a freestanding kitchen in the middle of the ground floor, sparing its dado panelling, a shower room and loo in the basement, and a bathroom on the top floor. Shorn of their secondary leaves, the first-floor shutters were glued back. 'Gluing is even worse than nailing,' Dan mutters darkly. He carefully unstuck them and had the missing leaves remade.

When Dan arrived he took slow stock of his new quarters. A friend advised him to sleep in every room to find his favourite, which he did. Little did he know that he would spend the next eight years working from room to room, discovering missing partitions, doors and panelling, and putting them back in their rightful places; faithfully copying and reinstating missing mouldings; repairing plaster, fixing shutters. He even found a grate buried in the back yard, minus its ribbed cheeks. Those were still in the fireplace in one bedroom and were a perfect fit.

There was an original lath-and-plaster ceiling in the drawing room and old plaster on other walls. 'Right from the start, I was determined not to take down any original plaster,' he says. But where he found impermeable modern concrete render causing damp, he removed it.

Repair work began in the drawing room, which had a few bits of panelling and an original impressive box cornice left. Supported by the expertise of the Spitalfields joiner Dave Thompson, he slowly copied and completed the panelling. His carpentry skills,

PREVIOUS PAGES Leftovers of panelling; bits of old wood from church pews, from the street and from friends, all carefully kept for use.

OPPOSITE, LEFT The iron-railed frontage of the 1775 sea captain's house of soot-darkened London stock, wreathed in mature climbing roses planted in the 1970s. Painting the woodwork in dark brown oil paint was historically apropriate.

OPPOSITE, RIGHT A view down to the yard, where original flagstones were found beneath two layers of later ones, along with a grate, restored to the front bedroom where its cheeks sat waiting; and black terracotta Victorian edging that now decorates the garden.

LEFT The distinctive coppery-green vestigial lead paint on the tongue-and-groove lining the stairs to the basement is so attractive that it has been left. The pieces came from an old village hall in Wales which had stripped them out.

which he had continued to develop, came into play as he worked out what went where.

'Box cornices are just that,' he explains. 'This one had four deal sections, two parts making a timber box, so the structure is actually hollow.' The beautiful old plaster ceiling was smothered by layers of Anaglypta wallpaper. Bit by bit he removed it with warm soapy water, a flexible filling knife, and 'a very sore neck'. That took three months, after which the hairy plaster was repaired by a specialist plasterer. In other places, distempered lime plaster had been covered with hard gypsum plaster, which Dan removed achingly slowly with a flexible knife, scraping and

prising, sometimes to be rewarded by glimpses of bright blue or orange distemper beneath. 'It's amazing that it was still there, behind the layers, waiting to be found,' he says. 'The thing is, you can't undo fifty years in a week. The work is very slow, but it is a thrill, not a chore. I love finding out how things work, and I enjoy the conservation side.'

He replaced the missing partition dividing the drawing room from the small back room. Its large double doors had been cut up and repurposed around the house as cupboard doors, so with the joiner's help he put them back together and reinstated them. Patching, then waxing the floors made the rooms gleam.

On the top floor, the former owners had taken out the partition because it had rotted. They'd bought a maple dance floor from Poplar and set it straight on top of the floorboards. Beneath it Dan found the original boards. And beneath those he lifted for repair he discovered hints of past owners. One had left a paper inscribed with ship lading-weight calculations; another hem-weights, perhaps from a curtain they were making; and someone must have been annoyed to lose a halfpenny, dated 1805. Hair pins and graphite drawing sticks had also slipped between the cracks. 'Along with a half a ton of dust,' Dan adds. Remarkably, from paint marks left on the old

OPPOSITE The elegant drawing room is a world away from how it was, with the chimney wall bare brick, much panelling and cornicing lost, the shutters glued back, and the original plaster ceiling buried under layers of wood-chip paper.

BELOW, TOP LEFT With its fire surround and overmantel panelling copied from similar houses and the whole unified with a soft, warm grey, the drawing room has a restful focus, set with brass candlesticks, an auction-bought still life and an unhung candle box.

BELOW, BOTTOM LEFT From among many items found under the floors, ranging from graphite drawing sticks to hem weights, emerged this rubbed halfpenny, with the profile of George III and dated 1805.

BELOW, RIGHT The doors that divided the drawing room from the dining room behind had been cut up and used as bits of cupboards all around the house. In the one shown here, neatly reassembled and given a weighty brass rim-lock, a split panel only adds to the attraction.

floorboards he identified the colours of the partition wall, much of which was in pieces in the loft. 'I carried them around the house, then one day saw that their colours exactly matched paint-marks on the floor. That was exciting.'

After seven years working his way through the house, it was remaking the beautiful basement kitchen and pantry that gave him most pleasure. He found vestiges of the old sink at the back, with a disconnected lead pipe heading towards the long-buried cesspit. Otherwise, concrete had been poured at some point; he left this *in situ*, but laid reclaimed handmade red quarry tiles on top.

Dan recalls his grandmother's kitchen in a sixteenth-century cottage near Deal, in which a huge Rayburn stove belted out

hot water as well as heat for cooking. The impressionable boy thought the range was 'like a huge living thing'. His grandmother had a quarry-tiled floor, limewashed walls, and kitchen chairs inherited from her own grandparents, two of which now sit at Dan's kitchen table, which he treasures.

Repairing and restoring the basement took almost a year and a half, working at nights and weekends alongside his day job. But now it is a place of purpose and serene beauty. The charming kitchen that Dan designed and built, painted ochre yellow, is set off by lime-plastered and limewashed walls. Behind a panelled screen painted in a delicious chocolate colour are a walk-in pantry and beside it, another small room for fridge and washing

machine. A rebuilt 1950s Aga takes pride of place in the large front hearth. The back area, with its roaring fire and an English dresser, makes a comfortable place to sit and relax – a pleasure and reward that Dan richly deserves.

OPPOSITE Partly glazed service cupboards run down one side of the kitchen, beneath stripped and cleaned joists. Assembled from many hoarded and repurposed doors and windows, supplemented with some pieces newly cut and painted brown, they contain a yellow ochre walk-in pantry and wine-storage room, as well as a utility room which also holds the refrigerator, allowing the kitchen itself to be uncluttered. A dresser is just visible in the back room.

BELOW The basement was the project that took longest. A thick concrete floor had been poured, so reclaimed red quarry tiles were laid on top. The look is based on Dan's grandparents' kitchen in a sixteenth-century cottage near Rye. The two chairs at the scrubbed plank preparation table belonged to a great-great-grandmother. Beside a fifties Aga, belting out warmth, is a stack of secondhand pans. Against the windows a practical butler's sink was set into a run of cupboards and drawers beneath a reclaimed iroko worktop.

OPPOSITE The view from the restored kitchen at the front through to a serene room in the back part. After the walls had been made good following the removal of concrete render, and allowed to dry out, they were lime-plastered by a master plasterer, then limewashed. The distinctive tone and texture work in harmony with natural materials such as wood, terracotta and earth colours to make a successful whole. The eighteenth-century carver chair and a provincial oak stool add to the slighty rustic, picturesque look.

BELOW Nothing beats a roaring fire. Old houses have often had their fireplaces reduced or blocked, which affects proper air circulation, and this house was no exception. One basement fireplace had been reduced using breeze blocks, with old newspapers stuffed in the cracks. Both were reopened to their original size and mended as necessary. In the back room a master builder built a plain hob-grate using iron bars found in the back yard. An alcove cupboard rebuilt with salvage is handy.

OVERLEAF Watery glass in the pantry reflecting cheerful flames; rose-leaf shadows on the door; it could be 1775 again.

BELOW LEFT Delft tiles make a splashback behind the basin, which has recycled, stripped old brass taps. The circular mirror reflects the cistern, which was secondhand and sand-blasted, set above a mahogany-seated lavatory (not shown).

BELOW RIGHT The glamorous brass and copper rainwater-head shower came from South Africa and had to be stripped and reassembled. Set against brick-shaped Edwardian-style tiles, with an unfussy shower-rail Dan made himself, it makes the most of a steel bath that, along with the washbasin and lavatory, was a bargain £100 (which shows the sense of reusing good-condition old fittings).

OPPOSITE This former swan-neck gasolier, proabably from outside a pub, has been converted to electricity and looks right unshaded. Its rusty metal complements the plain mirror frame and the flatted olive-drab panel behind, brushmarks nicely visible. A cloth at the window adds a flare of colour.

AN ARTIST'S LIFE

Getting to grips with an 1812 house in Whitechapel

PREVIOUS PAGES A small oak desk, a gift from a Dutch friend, a knackered Anglepoise found on the street in Ladbroke Grove, a scrap of embroidered linen against the light and some shutters given by the builder. These are the stuff of a writer's dreams.

LEFT The barren yard was covered in pink concrete tiles and builders' rubble. The African smoke bush, fig tree (not visible) and echiums were gifted as babies. Reclaimed flags laid to dirt allow the soil to breathe. In this small 1812 extension, rebuilt after being bombed, a flap of recycled mahogany makes an ad hoc writing or potting desk. The French pewter barometer was another gift.

OPPOSITE On the only west-facing window in a north–south aligned house, strong sunlight must be harnessed. Bits of tongue-and-groove found in a street in Hampstead have been cut to length, backed with rubber and placed against the astragals to make potting shelves for – in this case – young *Nicotiana sylvestris* grown from last year's seed. Fourteen trees are shoehorned into this pint-pot, organically gardened space. The small yard likes to think it is Versailles.

The joy of being an artist is – you're not afraid of having a go. When you're painting a picture, you mix colours instinctively and learn over time which combinations make what – like the first time I mixed a certain sharp yellow into black and got a Georgian sort of chrome green. It didn't quite make sense and it still fascinates. Nonplussed, I painted the shed door with it. Even so, I always found the colour disconcerting, and wherever I see that particular green I still do. To my mind, very strong green somehow belongs to grass and leaves, just as intense blue belongs to sky and water. In terms of painting inside a house, I've always felt that these colours should be used sparingly, particularly in their strongest incarnations, in which there is little if any white, except to provide body. In those lusty forms they seem so distinctly colours that belong to nature rather than to

inside. Of course they can still be used indoors, but they are best used knowingly, to create an effect.

In decorating terms, colours naturally suitable for daily use to offset things and people well are the off-whites and creams; the buffs and sludges and drabs; the warm deep earth-yellows and ochres; and some browns, as noted elsewhere in this book. Made from materials such as earth or rock or bones, they have a natural affinity with living things and are easy on eye and mood. Nevertheless, for rarer, more exciting and stimulating use, reds can work well indoors. Those famously so-called eating-room reds, perhaps seen first in China, perhaps spontaneously tried in Europe, cast a rich, warm, pleasant glow on pale skin, particularly when candle-lit. Not only do their historically expensive pigments indicate special rooms, but they add mystery

and occasion. Georgian pinks and rich salmons have a similarly pleasing effect – and all necessitate some costly red in the mix. Painted over a white ground they reflect and refract glowingly.

I bought a house at auction in 2005. I had saved for ten years and the fourteen-foot-wide derelict house was all I could afford. I had always longed for a garden but never had one. I longed too for a home to paint and furnish and cherish. The Regency terrace cottage had been boarded up for a decade, then squatted in, so was in a horrible state. Worse, it had been stripped. The only door left was the broken front door and there were only a few bits of skirting board. All the fire surrounds had been ripped off except a small Victorian metal one, and hearths in need of repair had been boarded over, much as a child hides something by shoving it in a cupboard, hoping no one will look.

The first thing was to let the house dry out, then to repair and clean the floorboards by hand, and remake doors and skirts. Fortunately, my derelict house was one of four built together in a group, probably by the same builder. Some still had original doors, so it was possible to take a pattern. The doors were remade with pine, just as would have been done in the past, though old pine was stronger. There is no MDF in this house, and hand tools were used where possible. I searched for latches and catches, particularly rim-locks and small brass knobs. Some were antique, some new but made in the old way, and none large or flashy, because this began as a small, poor house.

I designed a very plain freestanding kitchen against just one wall, with jointed doors and basic timber carcases. The fireplaces were unboarded, and where needed their overs repaired by a

master bricklayer who also rebuilt the garden wall where it had collapsed, using reclaimed bricks. I used lime mortar to match what was there. For the tall back wall, which was daubed with obscenities, I mixed a paint-kettle of limewash tinted with French yellow ochre artists' pigment.

There must once have been a garden, but now there were higgledy-piggledy pink concrete squares, mercifully plonked straight on to dirt, with heaps of builders' waste dumped on top. After clearing it I planted my first garden by trial and error. As it settled in, birds and bees returned, winging and thrumming. I also laid reclaimed eighteenth-century slabs, the crankiest of which I was told came from outside Samuel Johnson's house. That may or may not be true, but what a wonderful idea.

OPPOSITE The kitchen was designed as simply as possible, with a 1926 chemistry lab top, a gift, as a worktop (it glows with teak oil). A cupboard from Golborne Road makes cool storage in the hearth. All the cupboards are painted in a cheap mix of mainly earth pigments, giving a donkey-poo colour. The sturdy oak fin-de-siècle table is useful, and whether or not mirrors double space, they certainly help in a basement. Brass bib taps bespoke with an extra-long projection are a must to prevent the wood around the sink rotting.

BELOW This group of a melon, a large gourd and lemons rests on a fruit bowl turned from a burled tree trunk whose bark edges the turner was about to smooth off. Not everything has to be perfect to be naturally beautiful. When polished, the old copper kettle makes a fascinating contrast with the modern steel hob (kitchens need to work hard as well as look pretty).

Once the house had been patched up, I began painting it. I freely admit that apart from the hall mural, which took a long time, none of the other walls are very well painted. Unlike with easel painting, I paint walls fast, making no claim to an immaculate finish. A good finish is important on exterior woodwork, for there paint's principal function is to protect. Indoors, painting is more aesthetic. (Having said that, paint helps protect plaster against knocks and marks, while limewash, soft distemper, and casein paints all allow evaporation, and limewash discourages both vermin and some mould.)

I mix many of my own colours. It is cheaper and makes them unique, and I don't like having what anyone else has. But shortcuts are taken; I often use store-bought white as a base. The hall mural ground is a branded blue, but I mixed a cadmium-yellow glaze to brush over the top, so it looks evanescent and patchy, and is impossible to match (which I suppose is a form of snobbery). I based the design on scraps of hand-painted eighteenth-century wallpaper, a Chinese import featuring peonies and unfamiliar birds done in a distinct way, clearly by highly disciplined artists. While that took months to draw and complete, blossom by blossom, the small mural in the loo off the garden room is bravura and took a morning.

For the dining room red I used artist's paint. I had decided on red, but of those I mulled over in the art shop this one was on offer. I thinned it then slapped it on, ragging and battering it out with an enormous bristle brush for maximum spread. It is energetic work. If you don't tape and mask sufficiently, red-splotched casualties are inevitable over a surprisingly wide area.

OPPOSITE The low-celinged small dining room seats eight at a pinch. When these houses were built people were shorter and thinner. The red colour is artist's paint, applied fast with a big brush to give nice marks. The curtains, made from two cotton dresses, are hung on cup hooks from a garden cane; the seat is a tool chest.

LEFT Painting things a unifying dark colour can work wonders, as with the wooden fire surround here, painted black with a bit of red in it to make a very dark brown to match the carved panel above. The table has been set with salvaged Chinese export plates, a glass fruit bowl from a junk shop and a decanter that cost a fiver. The substantial pew chairs were a moving-in gift.

LEFT Even in a small, un-grand house like this, it is important to make distinctions. A cutter was especially made for the architrave to the drawing room from an early-nineteenth-century pattern book, and it took five goes to mix a satisfactorily elegant pale grey. Sadly, the cornices had already been removed.

BELOW Bookshelves have been put wherever conceivable, but there are never enough. They make good soundproofing and if cut wide add display space. The original dividing doors had been ripped out, so folding timber ones were made. The metal Victorian fire surround was *in situ*, painted, and has been left as it is. A benefit of being a painter is that when you want a painting, you can paint one.

OPPOSITE Post beds look well in these old houses, though often their only good bits are the foot-end posts. A gift of a length of beautiful silk woven to an eighteenth-century brocade pattern stood rolled up in the corner for three years, before fitting inside the bed exactly. The paint was a cheap lot that had gone wrong. Always check those cans by the door in paint shops.

The brushmarks are intentionally visible, which enlivens things. Because the paint is translucent, another coat would just make unsightly darker patches. When it becomes sufficiently scuffed to irritate, I will repaint the room another colour.

The kitchen is a curious pale pink. I'd intended to knock back the glare of a tin of leftover white paint, so I was busy whipping in some thinned raw umber and yellow ochre with a garden cane. That fateful winter day had a bilious light in which the tone looked a trifle green, so I decided to add a squirt of clear artist's red to balance it. Impatient to get on, I aimed straight into the can. Too much shot out. Red is pernicious. I couldn't find the red worm to fish it out, so there was nothing to do but mix it in. And since, like Dan Lucas (see page 194), I hate waste, I gritted my

teeth and painted the kitchen with it. I have grown fond of it now.

There is a sort of moral here. When adding strong colour to a base colour, always thin it and mix it in very carefully. Ideally make a sample and take notes. As with baking, one skips or breaks rules at one's peril. But on balance there are worse things in life than a very pale pink kitchen, and the beauty of paint is that if the result is truly offensive, it can be painted over. In terms of gently repairing old houses, there are also principles that it is wise to follow; and just as with the red paint, less is, generally, more.

LEFT Above dado panelling painted in an unobtrusive light drab, a mural adds drama to the narrow hall. A splat-back chair sits on the landing, while an older chair rests its weary legs below, handy as a *vide-poches*.

BELOW The mural was based on an eighteenth-century hand-painted wallpaper fragment: a blue-grey ground with loose-petalled peonies and rare birds. After being sketched with chalk it was drawn with a brush, then painted bloom by bloom and bird by bird. This is time-consuming work, and it is sobering to imagine the conditions in which early painters had to turn it out at speed.

LEFT The bedroom doubles as studio, its ceiling so low that the easel hardly fits. Painting the picture of the cat was a challenge, because the huge frame hardly came up the stairs. But putting big things in small rooms is a good trick that defies the limits of space.

BELOW LEFT A wall painting must be appropriate to its setting. This bravura orange tree painted in the small loo off the garden room, on a grey ground, was done fast. Old shutters were cut up to make the cupboard, and a bit of gingham looks cheerful on dowels on the glazed door.

BELOW RIGHT Dead space above the landing harbours bookshelves supported by cast-iron Gothic-style brackets. A big painting done years earlier just fits – miraculously – beside it, while a hand-printed Indian cloth tacked over a length of net-curtain cord, attached using cup hooks, colourfully curtains the window.

GLOSSARY OF TERMS

The history of materials and of paints used in old houses from the seventeenth century onwards is fascinating and complex, and has been widely researched and written about by numerous scholars and scientists in detail.

BEESWAX POLISH: The Society for the Protection of Ancient Buildings (SPAB) gives an excellent recipe for making wood polish from beeswax and turpentine. It keeps well when made and then stored in a clearly labelled jam jar.

BEAD AND BUTT: a type of **TONGUE-AND-GROOVE** decorative panelling made of lengths of timber, generally softwood that is often painted afterwards, which interlock by means of a tongue on one side and a groove on the other. In bead and butt, a bead runs along one side of the edge with the tongue.

CASEIN PAINT: Made with skimmed milk or whey, whiting (crushed chalk), linseed oil and slaked lime. Not particularly common; a forerunner of oil-based emulsion; and it can smell. Bristow (see Further Reading, opposite) provides a recipe.

CROWN GLASS: Glass was blown into a balloon, then a rod attached and the glass spun into a huge disc with great expertise. The outer areas were cut into panes; the central disc, with a knob left by the 'punty' rod, was used in cheap windows. No longer made. **CYLINDER GLASS** is probably the best approximation. A long cylinder is blown, slit down its length and flattened, causing a few ripples and the odd small elongated bubble. Also known as muff glass.

DISTEMPER (SOFT DISTEMPER): A once popular water-based paint made from a base of whiting soaked in water to make a white pigment, which is bound with size (glue such as rabbit-skin glue), and if desired coloured with pigment/s tolerant of alkalinity. Cheap and water-soluble, so it is only suitable for indoors use. Historically widely used to colour plaster, but also wood including panelling and doors. Gives a velvety matt finish. Note: the term 'distemper' generally refers to soft distemper. The alternative is oil-based distemper, which is much less common.

FAIENCE: A French term for fine tin-glazed earthenware. **MAJOLICA** in Italy and **DELFT**-ware (whether Dutch or English) are similar finishes.

GYPSUM PLASTER: Made with gypsum (calcium sulphate), which is widely found across Europe. It makes a very hard plaster. **PLASTER OF PARIS** is made with a burnt version of gypsum.

HORTICULTURAL GLASS: A low-grade cheap glass used in greenhouses. Often has flaws, which can be appealing.

LATH and PLASTER: Before the invention of plasterboard, walls and ceilings were usually plastered on to a substrate of riven (split along the grain) laths, usually made of chestnut, oak or Baltic fir carefully nailed to a timber supporting structure in a time-consuming process. The technique is still used in restoration and repair, and is also regaining popularity with traditionalists. Plaster applied correctly in this way can last for centuries.

LEAD WHITE and **OIL PAINT**: In a fairly complex process known since antiquity (the earliest known written account is by Vitruvius), white lead carbonate formed the traditional white base for oil-based or oil paint. Mixed usually, but not always, with linseed oil to form an opaque white paint that can be coloured, it is the basis for so-called lead paint. Lead white is toxic, therefore modern oil paints substitute either Zinc White or Titanium White.

LIME, LIME PLASTER, HAIRY or HAIRED PLASTER, LIMEWASH: When ground chalk (calcium carbonate), or other ground limestone is burned it makes lime, also known as quicklime (calcium oxide). Slaked with water, this becomes slaked lime (calcium hydroxide), called **LIME PUTTY**. On exposure to carbon dioxide in the air, it hardens (sets). All forms of lime are caustic. Limewash is a very dilute solution of lime putty. **LIME MORTAR** and **LIME POINTING** are made by mixing lime with sand, plus water, or mixing lime putty with sand. Lime plaster is essentially the same recipe but contains animal hairs – traditionally either horse or goat – for flexibility, and is also referred to as hairy or haired plaster. Experienced traditional plasterers and bricklayers have their own refinements on recipes and techniques for making and applying these breathable and flexible materials.

RED OXIDE PAINT: Historically this was made of lead oxide, which is red, mixed with oil, to produce a cheap, durable and protective paint coat sometimes also used as an undercoat. Today's versions do not use lead but strive for protective qualities.

SCAGLIOLA: An imitation stone or marble, realistic or fantasy, made from plaster, pigment, and glue, moulded to the required form, then polished or varnished.

STUCCO: Smooth plaster on the outside of a building carefully incised with lines to create the impression of much more costly stone blockwork.

WHITING: Finely crushed or powdered chalk (calcium carbonate) forming a base for water-soluble paints such as distemper. Sometimes referred to as Spanish White. For oil-based paints, lead white was used.

FURTHER READING

Baty, Patrick, *The Anatomy of Colour: the Story of Heritage Paints and Pigments*, Thames & Hudson, 2017.

Bristow, Ian C., *Interior House-Painting Colours and Technology, 1615–1840*, published for The Paul Mellon Centre for Studies in British Art by Yale University Press, 1996.

Hunt, Roger and Marianne Suhr, *The Old House Handbook: A Practical Guide to Care and Repair*, published in association with The Society for the Protection of Ancient Buildings by Frances Lincoln, 2008.

Mayer, Ralph, *The Artist's Handbook of Materials and Techniques*, Faber & Faber, 4th edition 1987.

Parissien, Steven, *Interiors: The Home Since 1700*, Laurence King Publishing, 2008.

The Society for the Protection of Ancient Buildings (SPAB) website offers excellent advice and information on a wide variety of subjects, technical guides that can be downloaded, and invaluable leaflets.

BELOW Never throw things out just because they are old. The hand-painted clock face in the garden room has no workings or hands but is still lovely, as are the dilapidated works of Charles Dickens, thier spines curiously faded a much prettier colour than the original red.

FRONT COVER In 'The Smallest House in the Street', a mahogany-framed convex mirror captures and encapsulates the sitting room, charging it with mystery and more than a dash of romance.

BACK COVER Now the grandest street in the area, stately Fournier Street concludes with Hawksmoor's masterpiece Christ Church, Spitalfields.

ENDPAPERS A large fragment of 1885 roller-printed wallpaper by Arthur Sanderson, the colours still fresh, was part of a cache found in the house described in 'What Lies Beneath'.

HALF-TITLE PAGE In the kitchen of 'A Conversation Piece', light and water shimmer on an ancient copper double sink. Neither steel nor porcelain comes anywhere near it for beauty.

TITLE PAGE In 'A Connection with the Past', distinctive effects created by time and life hold lost skills within them, as in a hand-forged butt hinge fixed with its original nails, and the paint layers around it, each with a story to tell.

CONTENTS PAGE In 'The Paintmaker's House', the sympathetic textures and colours of roughly glazed stoneware, japanned tin, painted pine and dishes heaped with fruit, all lifted by blossom, make this still life a feast for the senses.

PIMPERNEL PRESS LTD
www.pimpernelpress.com

Restoration Stories
© Pimpernel Press Limited 2019
Text © Philippa Stockley 2019
Photographs © Charlie Hopkinson 2019
Design by Becky Clarke Design

A catalogue record for this book is available from the British Library.

ISBN 978-1-910258-41-5

Typeset in Adobe Garamond and Gotham
Printed and bound in China by C&C Offset Printing Company Limited

10 9 8 7 6 5 4 3 2 1